D0566213

Provided to Kitsap Regional Library through donations from Heronswood Nursery visitors.

The Abundant Garden

A CELEBRATION OF COLOR, TEXTURE, AND BLOOMS

BARBARA J. DENK ～ **DEBRA PRINZING**

FOREWORD BY DANIEL J. HINKLEY

COOL SPRINGS PRESS

NASHVILLE, TENNESSEE

To the memory of

our dear friend and

much-admired gardener

Anne Clark Holt

July 24, 1925–July 23, 2004

Photography copyright © 2005 Barbara J. Denk

Text copyright © 2005 Debra Prinzing

Foreword copyright © 2005 Daniel J. Hinkley

All rights reserved. No part of this book may be reproduced or transmitted in any form, or by any means, electronic or mechanical, including photocopying, recording, or by any information storage and retrieval system, without permission in writing from the publisher.

Published by Cool Springs Press, a Division of Thomas Nelson, Inc., P. O. Box 141000, Nashville, Tennessee 37214.

Library of Congress Cataloging-in-Publication Data

Denk, Barbara J.
      The abundant garden : a celebration of color, texture, and blooms / Barbara J. Denk, Debra Prinzing.
          p. cm.
      Includes index.
      ISBN 1-59186-162-4 (hardcover photo-essay : alk. paper)
      1. Landscape gardening. 2. Gardens. I. Prinzing, Debra. II. Title.
      SB473.D426 2005
      712'.6—dc22
                                                                2004026606

Printed in Singapore
10 9 8 7 6 5 4 3 2 1

Editorial: Marlene Blessing, Marlene Blessing Editorial; Ellen Wheat
Design & Typography: Elizabeth Watson

Cover: An abundant setting: The koi pond in Caren and David Anderson's garden is cool and inviting, thanks to a vibrant display of hardy tropical and lush foliage plants that surrounds it. Photograph © copyright Barbara J. Denk.

Contents page: The dense spikes of a deep orange ginger lily (*Hedychium* sp.) are contrasted against the peacock blue wall of Linda Cochran's garden. Photograph © copyright Barbara J. Denk.

Back Cover: In Alan Clasens and Jimene Smith's garden, a weathered cedar bench is hidden amid feather reed grasses and blue fescue, suggesting the look of a windswept coastal beach. Photograph copyright © Barbara J. Denk.

Cool Springs Press books may be purchased in bulk for educational, business, fundraising, or sales promotional use. For information, please email SpecialMarkets@ThomasNelson.com.

Visit the Thomas Nelson Web site at www.ThomasNelson.com and the Cool Springs Press website at www.coolspringspress.net

acknowledgments

In 1999, the journey to create *The Abundant Garden* began when Barbara started photographing some of her favorite gardens in and around her home on Bainbridge Island, Washington. We are especially grateful for the warm welcome and generous support she received from the owners (and their families) of nine spectacular gardens, including: Cassie and Doug Picha, Marj and Nick Masla, Donna White, Carol and Gene Johanson, Caren and David Anderson, Al Clasens and Jimene Smith, Linda Cochran and David Jurca, Liz and Peter Robinson, and the late Anne Holt and Brantley Holt. We thank each of these special people for sharing their stories with Debra as she wrote the text to this book. Special appreciation goes to two garden designers who also contributed their time and comments to several chapters: Jay Fossett and Terri Stanley.

During her early years as a photographer, Barbara received professional encouragement from Leah Clark, who first viewed and edited her work, for which she is indebted.

In 2001, Melissa Matterazzo, the publicist for Bainbridge in Bloom, introduced us. This casual encounter over a cup of tea launched the enthusiastic partnership of mutual admiration and appreciation that led to *The Abundant Garden*'s creation. Likewise, Constance Bollen, a friend and creative designer, liked our ideas well enough to introduce us to Marlene Blessing, who ultimately "birthed" this project.

We are thankful for the early support from Fred Albert, *Seattle Homes & Lifestyles,* and Abella Carroll and Hillary Black at *Romantic Homes,* for publishing three of the gardens as feature articles in the pages of their magazines.

Several gifted persons helped us formulate our editorial ideas and graphic style for the book, including designer and art director Marcy Stamper and editor Barbara Boardman. Without these two talented individuals, the reality of this book's publication would have been difficult to realize and we thank them both.

Our fantastic editor, Marlene Blessing, first viewed our photographs and read the preliminary outline in 2002. She gave us our title when proclaiming: "These gardens are so abundant!" Marlene continued to support our ideas and creative efforts for two years until bringing the project together for Cool Springs Press. We are so grateful for her talent, spirit, vision, sense of humor, and Herculean efforts.

Marlene put together an exceptional team to develop this book, each of whom we greatly appreciate, including copyeditor Ellen Wheat and designer Betty Watson, who passionately embraced our vision, worked under ridiculous deadlines, and made it all a glorious reality on the printed page. Thank you both so much.

The Cool Springs Press team has been delightful to work with, including Cindy Games and Lola Honeybone, who have poured their enthusiasm and energy into helping us market and promote *The Abundant Garden.* And thank you, Hank McBride, for believing in this project and trusting us to create it for you.

Barbara would also like to thank her family and many friends, who never doubted her ability to complete this garden journey. And most of all she thanks her son, Christopher, and partner, Bill Troy, for their complete and loving presence in her life. Also, she will be forever grateful for Debra, who made sweet her dream.

Debra would also like to thank her parents, Fred and Anita Prinzing, for instilling in her a love for writing and the belief that she can do anything she sets her mind to do. And most of all, she thanks her husband, Bruce Brooks, and her sons, Alexander Brooks and Benjamin Brooks, for giving her an abundant life filled with love and laughter.

contents

the spell of
abundant gardening

foreword by Daniel J. Hinkley

◄ A tapestry of roses, edged with deep blue-purple salvia, creates a blissful and bountiful scene in front of the turn-of-the-twentieth-century storage shed adjacent to Liz and Peter Robinson's garden.

▲ Clad in the pendulous leaflets of a Japanese wisteria, Caren Anderson's art studio occupies the heart of her garden.

How curious it has been for me to have witnessed the evolution and distillation of a Pacific Northwest gardening identity during the past two decades. Even more curious to have been caught up in its vortex and survived to tell this tale. This is not to suggest that the region did not possess a brawny horticultural conviction long before I began my observations. The Northwest garden has been significantly actuated by the inspirations of individuals who are no longer visible. It just so happens that I arrived in the Northwest at a time when a certain chemistry was primed to react.

In 1985, I had just completed an advanced degree in horticulture from the University of Washington. My first two years of university-based research on the western slope of the Cascades might be

▲ Flamboyant and coppery,
the plumes of pampas grass
(*Cortaderia* sp.) tower above
Linda Cochran's garden.
▶ Liz Robinson's vermillion-colored
Asian peonies (top) and Carol
Johanson's blood-orange poppies
(bottom) add eye-catching
bursts of color and form to their
respective landscapes.

Everywhere I

looked were the

most astonishing

things . . . camellias

and viburnums

possessed the

genius to blossom

in the depths

of winter.

compared to Harry Potter's first term at Hogwarts. Everywhere I looked were the most astonishing things, as magical to me as floating candles and levitating platters of dessert. Camellias and viburnums possessed the genius to blossom in the depths of winter. On a day in January during my first winter, I came upon *Mahonia* 'Arthur Menzies', clad in its fingery trusses of fragrant flowers, and watched an Anna's hummingbird sup its nectar. This Michigan-born, Zone 4 lad found himself bewitched by the most unexpected climate of the upper left-hand side of this country, and there seemed no antidote strong enough to unfetter its spell.

It seems rather odd to say, as it was not that long ago, that gardening in the mid-1980s bore no resemblance at all to what it is now. Rare plants *were* to be found, but only in the gardens of the elite, traded like baubles among the cognoscenti who had proven their worth. Even in the Puget Sound area, which has long enjoyed a tradition of aberrantly good garden centers—Wells-Medina, Swanson's, Molbak's, Bainbridge Gardens, and others—stocking a truly rare plant was a departure from the norm. I might be wrong in this regard: however, I recall a certain undercurrent of suspicion of anything beyond the usual.

Yet all of this was about to change at the time my partner, Robert Jones, and I purchased our first piece of land near Kingston,

Washington, for what would become Heronswood Nursery. Garden writer Ann Lovejoy, whose excited and precise prose would soon energize a colossal audience, was poised to jolt awake a receptive public with *The Year in Bloom*. The Northwest Perennial Alliance, birthed by a small group of local sages, would become a magnet and a means by which to disperse the garden gospel. In the last days of each June, Hardy Plant Study Weekends became *the* destination for the horticultural community. Plants were here. They were rad. They were now.

Not only had extraordinary plants arrived but, for many gardeners, the quest to discover how to coax from them their finest effects in the landscape soon drove these enthusiasts to a near-addictive state. A highly charged and notoriously competitive adventure commenced. All of this was ultimately to the benefit of the Northwest landscape. A little friendly competition is a good thing. It makes people think. It makes gardens good. And we began to make good gardens.

Yet it is an ever-refining process. I have always made the case that gardening—in fact any new recreation—is much like learning to ski. Your first time down the mountain slope is always going to be the most perilous—and the most exhilarating. In the end, however, mastering technique will make the process more gratifying. Examining our geographical distinctions, wherever we garden, and then learning to play ball in a vernacular spin, is the name of the game. Horticulture is no longer the process of forcing the cultivation of the wrong plant in the wrong place.

With the fine photography and equally well-crafted, intelligent text in *The Abundant Garden*, the spirit of the new Northwest landscape can be shared with gardeners everywhere. Within these pages, readers will be immersed in the gardening uprising in which I found myself when I first moved to Western Washington over two decades ago. Also, contained between the lines of text in this book is a plea for a better understanding of, and dedication to, our personal circumstance. Of all things that I have witnessed during my all-too-brief exposure to regional gardening, today's ready embrace of taking our cues from our local climatic conditions, combined with choosing appropriate plants and planting them in exciting ways, exceeds all expectations. Wherever this occurs, it is like magic.

———

DANIEL J. HINKLEY is the co-founder of Heronswood Nursery in Kingston, Washington. He is the author of *The Explorer's Garden: Rare and Unusual Perennials* (Timber Press) and is a much sought-after speaker in the horticultural world.

welcome to a
garden of abundance . . .

ABUNDANCE: (n.) 1. *a great or plentiful amount.* 2. *fullness or overflowing.*

The Abundant Garden is a tribute to personal passion and inspired design techniques that can transform any backyard into one that looks and feels bountiful. Through evocative photography and personal interviews with an extraordinary gathering of garden makers, *The Abundant Garden* embraces a style of profuse and plentiful garden design. This book celebrates the very spirit of ardent individuality to which beginning and veteran gardeners alike aspire.

The Abundant Garden encourages those who view the garden as a medium for artistic expression and provides beginning gardeners with useful steps for creating their own richly diverse landscape. It transports readers into the intimate world of nine special landscapes and the creative garden makers who tend them. Each place expresses a different style. Each has been designed with an appreciation for details, which for some gardens may be relaxed and for others quite formal. These landscapes convey distinct characteristics and personalities, yet there is a common design lexicon, a ribbon that weaves together each of their stories. Readers will be able to appreciate abundant garden design with fresh eyes, discovering ideas that will overflow into landscapes of their own.

Features of an Abundant Garden

"What is an "abundant garden"? "It means you can't see the dirt. Anywhere!" suggested one garden designer. "It's all about scale. The plants aren't wimpy," said another. Regardless of their design style or the plants chosen for them, abundant gardens share many characteristics. These aren't gardens where "more is more." In fact, well-designed abundant gardens are anything but excessive. They are not gardens where as many plants as possible have been crammed together in the ground. Neither are they about conspicuous consumption and the aspirations to grow as many rare plants as one can financially afford.

◄◄ Spring's abundance: blade-shaped forms of companionable plants create a pleasing repetition of patterns against a walled garden.

◄ Hot pink, a color often found in exuberant roses or perennial blooms, coats a pair of Adirondack chairs, adding a burst of raucous color against a calm lawn.

▲ A row of brick caps a concrete wall, bringing a touch of formality to a cottage garden.

▲ A carefree planting of summer perennials draws the eye toward a crisp, white clematis vine and a tidy picket gate.

When you enter an abundant garden, you're aware of its dimensional nature: plantings and structures create the sense of "walls," "ceilings," "windows," and "floors." Abundant gardens are thoughtfully grown, yet there's also something serendipitous about them. Mother Nature has her way in an abundant garden, embroidering that which human hands have formed with self-sowing plants and unexpected surprises.

Abundant gardens are inviting because of their largesse, even in the smallest of spaces. Foliage intermingles, forms interconnect, structures envelop, and each of the senses responds to being in an exceptional environment. Some abundant gardens are playful and carefree, while others are designed with a sense of horticultural order. Plant choices play a strong role in setting the tone: in one garden perennials are queen, while in another trees and shrubs take center stage.

Enter the world of abundant gardens and you'll enjoy a journey through a verdant, textured environment, populated by common and uncommon trees, shrubs, vines, ground covers, perennials, grasses, and bulbs. You'll travel along thoughtfully placed paths, or walkways that have evolved in a happenstance manner. You'll luxuriate in views near and far and take notes as you contemplate crafting your own abundant surroundings.

Who creates an abundant garden? The garden makers you'll meet in these pages live abundant lifestyles that flow into the garden at every opportunity, whether through play or work, solitude or entertaining, artistic expression or ecological stewardship. People who design and tend abundant gardens are zealous about their patch of earth; they bring a lively and improvisational approach to the art and practice of gardening. Those who create abundant gardens are anything but rigid when it comes to "rules" of design.

Where does an abundant garden grow? Abundant gardens present a profusion of texture, color, pattern, intimacy, spontaneity, and energy. Indeed, abundance is a universal theme that weaves through many of the world's most famous garden styles and locales. Each of the nine extraordinary gardens featured in this book grows and thrives on Bainbridge Island, Washington, a half-hour ferry ride from Seattle, to the west across Elliott Bay. The growing conditions on this horticulturally diverse island are widely varied, the design vocabulary is multifaceted (ranging from traditional to progressive), and the plant collections are mesmerizing.

Gardeners in this temperate locale describe it as the Northwest's "Mediterranean zone," with wet, relatively mild winters and rain-free summers. The microclimates on Bainbridge Island typically fall between USDA Zone 7b (average minimum temperatures of 5 to 10 degrees Fahrenheit) and Zone 8a (10 to 15 degrees Fahrenheit). During the summer months, it's not unusual for gardens to require ongoing supplemental irrigation; consequently there is an increasing interest in designing drought-tolerant gardens. These gardens illustrate how to plan, design, and cultivate an abundant garden, offering ideas that gardeners can adopt anywhere.

An abundant garden transcends aesthetics and horticulture. The essence of gardening is to create and nurture harmonious beauty in one's own private environment. A garden of abundance reflects passion and joy. It also reflects a generous spirit, one in which all physical elements—color, texture, form, and more—spill over the garden's pathways, arbors, gates, and containers within. It's our wish that you'll make use of many of the successful design ideas shown here. Regardless of the style or personality of your garden, you'll have a spirit of abundance when you abandon gardening according to rules, and instead cultivate a landscape that's grown from the heart.

Design Concepts

Many concepts and design styles help form a garden of abundance. Nine prevailing themes are introduced and discussed in *The Abundant Garden*. Yet these hallmarks appear to some degree in all of these unique landscapes, illustrating how well they work in tandem with one another. For each garden, we've singled out the most evident and fully realized concept it illustrates, These gardens express traits of many, if not all, of the abundant ideas outlined here:

Spontaneity: Nothing in an abundant garden looks contrived or unnatural. Plants, ornamentation, and architecture seem effortlessly combined. Highly personal, the expression of spontaneity can be as simple as placing a cherished ceramic pot among ferns, perching a tiny figure on a mossy stump, or intentionally bending a pathway so you can't see where it goes. Spontaneity in the garden is achieved when the unseen suddenly becomes visible, when discovering the unpredictable brings delight to the viewer. A light hand tends the plantings in an abundant garden. Eschewing the artificial, the keeper of an abundant garden encourages plants to follow their natural habits, training vines to cover inanimate structures and allowing a certain camaraderie to flourish where branches weave together, stems intermingle. As a result, there's an overall feeling that nature has expressed its beauty and artistry with exuberance.

Layering: Deep, overflowing borders that reflect the shape and proportions of a plant help bring the garden into scale with the home it surrounds. A garden of plants that grow true to their forms—not aggressively pruned or manipulated—looks and feels abundant. It's not wild, nor is it designed with a heavy hand. Edges are imprecise; spaces between paving stones are occupied by lush ground covers; plants follow their own natural form with staggered heights and varying habits. The concept of layering doesn't just relate to tidy rows of tall, medium, and low plants. Layering can be impressionistic, pieced together like a puzzle, with turns and curves that embrace like-minded plants nearby. As when composing a painting, the creator of an abundant garden places plants for maximum impact, layering for an equation that is greater than the sum of its individual parts.

Intimacy: When a garden offers its visitors secluded, half-hidden spaces, there's a sense that the public and private are linked. As you approach an enclosed space in the garden, you anticipate discovery. Once inside an intimate garden space, glimpses of the world beyond provide a human connection through windows or doorways, real or implied. This idea of a garden-within-a-garden offers quiet shelter and a place of rest, while echoing the greater environment in which it exists. Like yin and yang, the inner and outer spaces of a garden should interrelate. Enclosures contribute to this balance. Courtyards, sunken patios, partial walls, sections of fencing, rows of tall pots, living hedges, and filtered light through branches can communicate a sense of intimate enclosure. The suggestion of intimacy gives an abundant garden a deeper level of richness and energy—a private, interior life.

Framed Views: Like a frame artfully presenting a portrait, entrances and transition points in a landscape can showcase garden scenes, offering tantalizing glimpses of that which is within. By leading or directing those who arrive, portals (passages, gaps, and openings) orient the movement into, through, and out of a garden using view lines and staggered destinations. Determine the threshold of your garden and use it to clarify central elements, direct attention, or hint at something wonderful within. After identifying where the threshold is, the question of "shape" is also important. Is the framed view wide or narrow? Obvious or secretive? Arched and welcoming, or closed and mysterious? A narrow anteroom, formed by shrubs or structures, can lead to the garden's inner sanctum, distancing public areas from private ones. A bend in the path, a change in level, a narrowing of the space—all the ways space is framed help determine the mood of a landscape.

Ornamentation: When integrated with bold or finely textured foliage, gracefully arching grasses, or twining vines, garden ornamentation reinforces the feeling of abundance in a landscape. The ornamental element may be a piece of art, an architectural structure, or an eye-catching specimen tree, but each lures the viewer through a landscape. It's human nature to walk toward an implied destination. Be it the ultimate goal (for example, the front porch of a home) or an interim goal (a fountain, sculpture, or bench flanked by two trees), points of interest slow one down, resulting in more time spent in the garden. Well-placed ornamental pieces make for a satisfying journey along a path; when centrally placed, they can create the heart of a garden. Meandering, daydreaming, thinking, and contemplating while journeying from one artful point of interest to the next are the hallmarks of time spent in an abundant garden.

Movement: Rhythm provides the essential movement within an abundant garden, yielding byproducts of energy, animation, music, and sensations. In design terms, time and movement are partners in a rhythmic dance; balance and emphasis are their supporting cast. Dynamic movement provides a visual flow to the landscape. As a beat is to music, as choreographed steps are to a dance, the presence of movement in a garden adds vitality. Movement can be expressed by the intentional placement of fluid plants—grasses, ferns, or leafy vines—where they can capture a breeze. Movement can also be expressed using inanimate objects, making static materials come alive: evenly spaced paving stones, an undulating cascade of river rock, the repetition of like forms, each energizing the landscape.

Patterns: Abundant gardens have a vocabulary, and patterns are at the core of this language. Repetition, reflection, the play of light and shadow all conspire to link and connect, resulting in a balanced, cohesive environment. Patterns create the feeling of abundance as forms are repeated, materials are echoed, shapes are complemented, and objects change the way pools of light fall. Simple themes convey a pattern when used again and again in the landscape. Look for the dominant form in an abundant garden and you'll see it—consciously or unconsciously—repeated and reinforced throughout. Geometric or organic in nature, patterns are the building blocks of an abundant garden.

Color: Bright or subtle, the abundant garden has a vibrant palette. Warm, rich plant colors predominate in the landscape, offering a compelling counterpoint to a continuum of green shades provided by foliage (gray, blue, silver, gold, maroon-purple). Natural or painted wood, pigmented concrete, glazed pottery, and reflective or weathered materials—these, too, contribute to the palette of a garden. What's important in the selection and application of color in the garden is noting how it relates to natural light. Northern, cooler gardens may demand richer colors to command attention; Southern gardens, with a saturated radiance, may need a lighter touch. Color in an abundant garden enhances and defines space.

Timelessness: How does one grow a garden of abundance that seems to have been there forever? When we incorporate organic materials that suggest a sense of age and rich character into the garden—moss-encrusted stones, weathered wood, vine-covered trellises, and aged copper roofs—we can successfully communicate timelessness. With ingenuity and resourcefulness, many of these architectural features and materials can be incorporated into a landscape—with the suggestion that they were placed there years before. When it comes to using plants to create an atmosphere of timelessness, the strategy is trickier. Most of us can't afford to purchase mature trees, but we can borrow tricks from the masters: grouping several younger trees into an inviting stand or dense grove; planting layers of horizontal plants beneath vertical ones for textural depth; framing views of adjacent gardens, parks, greenbelts, or pastures; and directing a subtle play of light into the more intimate rooms of the garden. Achieving timelessness depends less on the passing of years and more on gaining an understanding of what plants and organic materials contribute to the garden.

garden getaway

a rustic rural garden

a rustic rural garden

When you tour Cassie and Doug Picha's pastoral family compound, you are encouraged to wander away from obvious pathways. Whether spread with crushed rock or soft wood chips, the paths here don't always have an obvious beginning or end. So it's fine with these hosts if visitors vanish through the opening in a border, wade barefoot into the pond, or are discovered napping in the hidden hammock. "I like giving a sense of spontaneity and mystery to my garden," Cassie says.

Theirs is a well-lived-in landscape, one that has accommodated everything from neighborhood softball games to a herd of grazing sheep. On twelve acres of land, some of which was once devoted to strawberry crops, this capable and creative couple has raised four

◄◄ Bountiful in bloom and generous in yield, the Picha kitchen garden nourishes both body and spirit.

◄ Housing tools, ducks, and chickens, the gray-shingled barn serves as a reminder of Doug's agricultural upbringing. Together, edibles and ornamentals thrive in nearby borders.

▲ A rusted and weathered iron tricycle appears unexpectedly near the lavender border.

▲ By adding two posts and a
wrought-iron swinging gate,
Cassie and Doug turned an already
abundant border into one that
embraces a spontaneous spirit.

There's a heightened
interest when organic
plant shapes are
contrasted with
salvaged finds and
rough-hewn structures.

children, grown hundreds of plants both edible and ornamental, and created a garden that reflects their horticultural interests and collecting passions. "This is very much a partnership," Cassie maintains. "We work together on the weekends—we're out in the garden a lot."

Typical of their embrace of the unexpected, she and Doug welcome rustic icons into their garden; they give utilitarian objects and aged tools a renewed purpose by displaying them among vibrant mixed borders and pumpkin vines. An old gas can is elevated to sculpture status. Recycled raspberry posts are paired with twisted branches to form an alluring arbor or a railing on a footbridge that leads to the pond. Handcrafted birdhouses have an important place here, too, as does a distressed iron gate to "nowhere." There's a heightened interest when organic plant shapes are contrasted with salvaged finds and rough-hewn structures. Elsewhere, romantic, overflowing borders reflect the Pichas' informal lifestyle.

That the energetic couple has invested so much time, money, and creativity into this landscape is due, in part, to their family ► 26

▲ Embellished with bent and twisted branches that form its balustrade, the rustic footbridge beckons visitors to cross, perhaps first peering over the railing to see their reflections in the pond below.

memorable beauty: planned and unplanned

Being spontaneous

takes practice.

One of my favorite ways to escape the stress of everyday life momentarily is to recollect unforgettable garden memories. It's a rewarding habit to cultivate. Some impressions provide comfort, while others prompt tears of joy. A whiff of gardenia instantly reminds me of my wedding day. Bright red geraniums in terra-cotta pots bring me back to the garden terraces I once admired on a trip to Venice. A flame-colored mosaic of autumn leaves transports me to my childhood in New England. These fleeting gifts of surprise and delight are what distinguish the most endearing of gardens.

If we yield to spontaneity in our gardens, we begin to see with new eyes and to listen for sounds that resonate with the spirit. What puts a smile on our faces? What interrupts our thoughts and commands our attention? A wry grin or the flutter of one's heart are obvious responses to an unexpected sight, scent, or sound in the garden. One famous gardener hid a motion sensor in his landscape so his visitors would unwittingly trip soothing music. A plantswoman I know has placed an angled mirror where her pathway reaches a dead end, adding a touch of intrigue to

the journey. The incongruous presence of a bowling ball and bowling pin, which coincidentally echo the hue of a nearby bloom, prompts a burst of laughter from visitors to Cassie and Doug Picha's garden.

Here are some of the memorable sights I've glimpsed: the undaunted performance of a rose that's still blooming in December; the split-second appearance of a tiny hummingbird, darting from one nectar-rich flower to the next; a sweet pea that's chosen to twine through the handle of a vintage watering can, carelessly abandoned by its owner.

When an area seems lifeless in a garden, perhaps you can take this as a hint to add an element of surprise. Being spontaneous takes practice. When we were young, playing in the mud seemed natural, but as we mature into adulthood, some of us find it hard even to get dirt under our nails. We can infuse our gardens with a lively, free-spirited attitude by tuning into clues around us and responding imaginatively to the seasonal changes that naturally occur.

The act of gardening and the pursuit of beauty are not mutually exclusive. Indeed, they're interdependent. When seasoned with a dash of spontaneity and playfulness, the result is an unforgettable garden destination.

▲ ▲ Salvaged from the property's past, an impromptu collection of metal objects.
◄ ▲ The raspberry-pink florets of this dahlia resemble an explosion of fireworks.
◄ A ruby bowling bowl is displayed on an ornamental pedestal.
► Vigorous and beautiful, the pink-flowered *Clematis montana* has a mind of its own.

They do see their rustic, rural property as a metaphor for how to live, love, and raise children.

heritage, Cassie explains. They moved here in the early 1980s, while she was pregnant with Teddy, their first child, now twenty-one. "Doug comes from three generations of farming families—he likes to get his hands dirty and sweat," she says. "And my grandfather was a dairy farmer."

Doug and Cassie haven't exactly recreated their childhoods by trying to earn a living from the land (he is an executive in the health-care field and she runs a garden design business). But they do see their rustic, rural property as a metaphor for how to live, love, and raise children. "We planted an English oak when the children were little, and it has grown with them," Cassie says, gesturing to a mammoth shade

▲ From top left: Espaliered apples; Gas can-as-artwork sits among the lacy fennel foliage.

◄ A vine-hidden birdhouse.

▼ From bottom left: the perfection of lilies and a glazed red birdhouse, adding a gloss to the humble scene; St. Francis appears to bless this garden.

▲ Supported by a teepee-style arbor, golden sunflowers convey the joy of summertime.

"Doug and I would sit down and draw out the lines of the garden on napkins to decide where the fences would go."

▲ ▲ The reproduction Italian birdbath adds a touch of formality to the border of geraniums.

▲ A post supports both birdhouse and clematis vine.

tree at the edge of the lawn. "Like raising children, you have to be patient and flexible when growing a garden." With sons Teddy and Joe pursuing their college studies in California, only two Picha children live at home these days: daughter Allie, seventeen, and youngest son Sam, fifteen.

With many sections of their property still populated by second-growth Douglas firs and western red cedar trees, Doug and Cassie have been careful to retain as many wooded areas as possible. For example, they cleared hundreds of alder saplings that had grown unchecked in order to make room for the home's foundation, but they also retained a thick greenbelt of original trees that lines all four sides of the property's perimeter. "Doug and I would sit down and draw out the lines of the garden on napkins to decide where the fences would go," Cassie recalls of those early years on the property, when the young family lived here in a mobile home.

By the late 1980s, once they'd settled into a comfortable, two-story, gray-and-white-trimmed farmhouse, Cassie and Doug laid out the garden's main sections. They established an orchard with sixty fruit trees, a kitchen garden measuring twenty-five-by-eighty feet, a rustic, fifty-foot-long pergola, dahlia beds, lavender borders, and mixed plantings around their home. They dug a pond in a boggy area and marked off the baseball field.

The kitchen and cutting garden thrives just beyond the back door, perfectly situated for grabbing a few herbs or tomatoes for a family meal. Cassie designed the surrounding latticework fence with an arbor-covered opening, now clad with a golden hops vine. She finished the wood with Cabot's bleaching oil to give it a grayish, weathered appearance. Inside the fence, there is no shortage of happily adjusted plants, herbs, roses, vines, and vegetables—most of which display an uncontained habit as they spread up and over the edges of raised beds, reaching through the fencing and out onto the lawn. A six-by-eight-foot glass greenhouse occupies one corner of the enclosed kitchen garden, providing Cassie a place for tender plants to overwinter. "I especially love to be in the greenhouse on a rainy day in spring," she enthuses.

Many of the trees and shrubs that Cassie began planting fifteen years ago are reaching mature stature. "They provide an understory that grows beneath the layer of conifers; the ornamental trees are enhanced by that canopy of evergreen," she points out. Sourwood (*Oxydendron arboreum*), smoke tree (*Cotinus coggygria*), empress tree (*Paulownia tomentosa*), the gold form of black locust (*Robinia pseudoacacia* 'Frisia'), flowering dogwood, and weeping willow provide a well-structured framework with multiseason interest.

According to Cassie, everything that grows here has had to endure the wear and tear of a large family. "There's a poor Japanese maple that has been first base forever. And the lacrosse balls are always flying into the perennials."

Today Cassie is a sought-after garden designer whose company In the Garden Design typically works on three or four residential landscapes at once. But her journey toward gardenmaking was as irregular as her own garden's evolution. Prior to launching her landscape business in 1996, Cassie owned and operated a childcare center, and later a small gift-manufacturing business. ("I once spent a summer making seven thousand candles that I hand-painted in my garage," she recalls.) This combination of having a high metabolism and the urge to create serves Cassie well, both in her own home and garden, and on behalf of her clients.

Doug and Cassie are often spurred to new garden design innovations by urgent deadlines, such as the times when they've agreed to offer their garden as a scheduled stop on a summer garden tour. It's no surprise, says Cassie, that these commitments have resulted in some of the landscape's most prominent features, including the pond, a small footbridge, and the pergola, which Doug designed and built. ▸ **33**

▼ It's a barefoot kind of day, as Sam Picha plays with two of the family pets.
▼ ▼ Doug fabricated the inviting pergola with recycled poles and posts. The structure leads to a partially hidden garden bench.

planning
the element
of surprise

Allow deliberate design
elements to blend happily
with accidental ones.

A garden with a spontaneous spirit offers opportunities for wonder and awe around every corner. Surprises may be intentionally placed by the designer or they may appear at the hand of Mother Nature, but they all serve to delight the viewer and imbue the landscape with an upbeat, whimsical personality or a mysterious, magical quality.

When the unseen becomes the visible, when the unpredictable comes into focus, the garden reveals why we're drawn to nature in the first place. The desire to discover the hidden secret or the unexpected treasure is indeed the allure for many garden lovers.

Cassie and Doug Picha allow deliberate design elements to blend happily with accidental ones. They give equal status to both the ordinary and the rare: edibles are tucked among precious ornamentals; glossy finishes appear in contrast to rustic twig structures; lavish plantings occupy humble vessels. A spontaneous garden such as the

Pichas' gives the impression that its owners skipped away from garden tasks for an impromptu picnic, midway through the job.

To design for spontaneity is like telling a cautious person to lighten up. It can't be forced, but it can be achieved, little by little. One garden may reflect the "controlled chaos" of its owner's style, with wild-looking perennials surrounded by clipped boxwood hedges. Another garden may encourage vines, ground covers, and perennials to follow their innate habits and comingle for fantastic, unplanned results.

Such spontaneity is expressed by using plants, architecture, and artful ornaments.

Plants: A joyous celebration of plants— their unique traits, forms, habits, and blooms—adds up to a garden with a charismatic and engaging attitude. When plantings are slightly askew, not rigidly groomed or contrived, their informality is appealing. Self-sowing plants appear where they're least expected, peeking through openings, filling cracks, and scrambling over

sculptures. Bloom and foliage colors may clash for surprisingly successful pairings like orange and pink or yellow and black. You can challenge conventions and pair common annuals with exotic bulbs, or train floriferous vines into the branches of ornamental trees.

Architecture: Continue the sense of spontaneity with structures, furnishings, and pathways. Design with a light hand, giving arbors, fences, and gates an imperfect, unpolished quality that blends comfortably with the natural environment. Many constructed elements have an inherent purpose, but they also invite adornment— finishes and accessories that infuse a utilitarian object with humor or whimsy. Juxtapose the unanticipated with the expected, such as hanging a salvaged window from the fence, or placing a bench where you can't quite see its legs among the perennials. Impose a jog in the path so you can't see its

▲ Saved from the junk heap, this paned
window frames a garden view.

terminal point. Erect a gate that lures exploration to what's hidden, just beyond.

Artful Objects: When design elements coexist with upbeat plantings or riotous blooms, their impact is indelible. A grouping of mismatched containers has its place in the garden, communicating an offhanded gesture of fun. Frivolous accents in astonishing places cause the viewer to stop and notice their presence. An unconventional placement of found objects never fails to surprise, especially if it reflects the designer's hobbies, collections, and interests.

When a garden displays a spontaneous mood, whether by intent or by happenstance, when artistic freedom is encouraged and design rules are broken, we are drawn to the appealing result.

▼ In addition to weathered cedar and chipped paint, rust is the one of the preferred finishes in this garden. The obelisk-topped stake stands amid a mixed border of roses and lamb's ears.

► The leaves of a golden hops (*Humulus lupulus* 'Aureus') and grapevine create a screen to shelter those who sit in this bench-and-arbor structure.

▼ The irregularly shaped pond has lush borders populated by moisture-loving plants.

Always one to see the inherent beauty and value in weathered and timeworn materials, Doug created the inviting pergola using scrap cedar poles that he salvaged from the property. He fashioned its arborlike roof from discarded posts that he collected from raspberry farms around the island. The structure draws visitors from the street-facing side of the Picha property, where Doug grows his favorite dahlias and tends to beds of squash and pumpkins. It continues behind the barn that houses fifteen chickens and five ducks, and emerges near the aromatic lavender borders.

Other than providing a wonderful, slightly crooked journey for their guests, the pergola serves as the place Doug hangs a growing assortment of metal objects he's discovered half buried on the property. "Anything that harkens back to the island's early days of farming and his boyhood memories gets showcased," Cassie claims. "His finds can be a bucket full of rusty nails, old tools, pulleys, pieces of metal fencing. I have to restrain him from going to the dump to find more!"

Most of the plants growing here have minds of their own, making time the most constant challenge for Cassie and Doug. "Since we started with such vast spaces, I realize that I have been the 'Queen of Overplanting' as I just tried to fill in this garden," Cassie says. Occasionally, there is editing to be done, when Cassie has to remove overgrown trees, like a big-leaf maple that shaded out too many other plants.

She appreciates the lighthearted spirit of her garden, even in places where she can't always weed regularly. "One of the things I bring to the table for my clients is that I have grown so many different plants, including every self-sower possible," maintains Cassie, revealing her contagious enthusiasm. Foxglove, bronze fennel, hardy geranium, and California poppies are among the many resident plants in her garden that pop up without any human encouragement.

From the garden's tamer, cultivated plantings to the wild areas around its edge, there's always a living vignette that reveals Doug and Cassie's affection for this place. This is where chores are followed by an afternoon of lounging in an Adirondack chair or dozing in the hammock. And backyard stargazing occupies a few moments of the evening.

Despite the hard work required to maintain their large and varied garden, Cassie and Doug can't imagine being anywhere else. They're often reminded of this conviction at day's end. "We were drawn to this property because we could still see the strawberry furrows from the farm that was once here," Cassie recalls. "We still love sitting outside and watching the sky at dusk; there's a silhouette that forms over the tops of the cedars—it's like looking at a mountainscape." ❧

"Anything that harkens back to the island's early days of farming gets showcased."

▼ Containers filled with heat-loving summer annuals and tropical cannas decorate the back steps of the Picha house.

▼▼ Dark purple water irises thrive along the pond's edge.

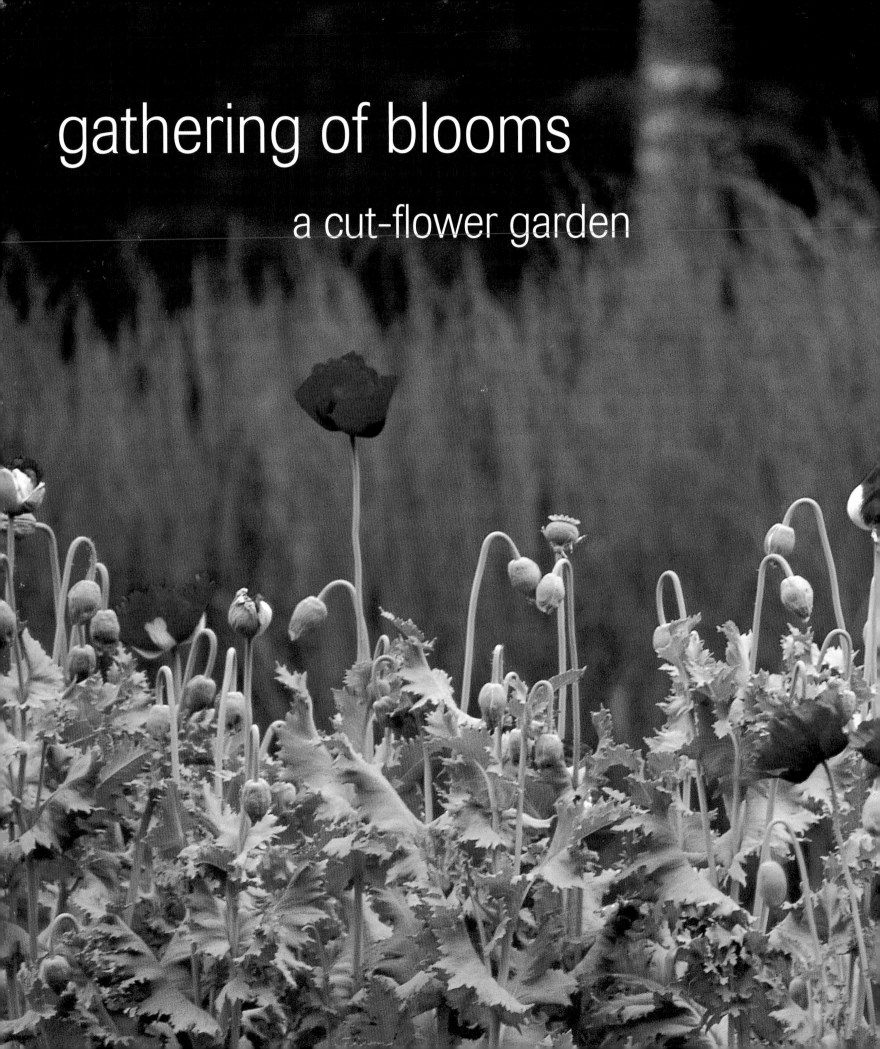

gathering of blooms

a cut-flower garden

a cut-flower garden

◄ ◄ Two forms of annual poppies, a red-and-white 'Danish flag' and an unnamed salmon form, have cross-pollinated to produce a new poppy in the Masla garden. Nick describes it as "red, with purple-black splotches." The poppies bloom in front of feather reed grass (*Calamagrostis* x *acutiflora* 'Karl Foerster').

▲ The Masla family's cut-flower stand invites customers to create their own bouquets.

Like a fiber artist who selects colorful threads and yarns to fashion a vibrant tapestry, Nick Masla chooses perennials and grasses to weave a multilayered landscape, blending them together in dynamic, textured compositions. Varied foliage and bloom shapes surround his home and occupy soil once home to thistle and weeds. Deep, overflowing borders are punctuated with towering accents of blue and magenta. "I like to plant billowy, rounded forms, and then have spikes shooting up through them—that's the bountiful look I'm going for," he explains.

With his wife Marj, Nick has spent more than fifteen years transforming a rundown parcel into 2.5 acres of cutting and display gardens. This is a do-it-as-you-go effort where, despite demanding

▲ Growing in front of a 4-foot-tall stand of oxeye daisies (*Heliopsis helianthoides* var. *scabra* 'Summer Sun'), a mass of red-blooming knotweed (*Persicaria amplexicaulis* 'Firetail') electrifies a deep border.

▲ Weekend floral designer Marj Masla creates complex bouquets using unusual choices grown by her husband, Nick.

▶ Nick Masla, weekend farmer, has turned a production cut-flower farm into an inviting and enticing display of colorful and textured borders.

▶▶ A painterly bouquet features fresh-cut blooms, straight from the Masla garden, including phlox, hydrangea, *Sedum* 'Autumn Joy', and white-blooming *Lysimachia clethroides*.

jobs and two school-age children, the Maslas have planned and planted masses of flowers for cut bouquets they sell to neighbors, friends, and regulars. "I love growing flowers and Marj loves arranging them," says Nick, a veteran public administrator who swears he was destined to be a farmer (at least on the weekends). His passion to cultivate unusual crops not typically found at florist shops stems from a childhood spent surrounded by Midwestern farmland. Heliopsis, helenium, perovskia, euphorbia, sedums, and countless other choices make their way from Nick's borders into the bouquets Marj creates.

Her original combinations incorporate perennials, annuals, grasses, and herbs—ingredients for bouquets sold at a curbside stand, a family endeavor involving John Masla, twelve, and Mary Masla, fifteen. ▶ **43**

► From top: Single flower favorites include 'Autumn Beauty' sunflower, 'King Arthur' delphinium, California tree poppy, and a summer dahlia.

layering

Terraces, slopes, and gentle or radical grade changes can enhance the success of a layered design.

By choosing plants with varying heights and habits and grouping them into a complex arrangement, you can give the garden a sense of unity and cohesion. "Layering" is the term often used to explain this process, one in which the garden's boundaries and edges are obscured. As a result, tiers and levels of plantings interact, moving the viewer's eye upward, across, and through a border or island to see a seamless composition rather than individual plants.

Layering as a design concept initially brings to mind an orderly, stair-step installation, such as planting taller choices at the back of the border, with medium-sized plants in front of them, finished off with ground covers or small perennials as the lowest or first layer. This method, perhaps inspired by floral design techniques, often reads flat rather than voluptuous.

The best layered gardens travel well beyond a linear starting point. Rather than going for high-contrast plant forms, the well-layered garden relies on a subtler scheme. Think of it as a watercolor painted with understated washes of color, rather than a bold contemporary canvas with high-contrast colors or shapes.

A garden's layers should not succumb to the reliable and usually uninterrupted lines of fences, walls, and the exterior of your home. Rather than having a bed or border echo a home's boxy perimeter, the best layers borrow from a nonlinear touchstone, such as the curve in a driveway or the arch of a fanlight window. If there isn't an archetype to inspire you, simply create a defining shape and repeat it whenever possible. Curves, arches, diamond patterns, and other geometric or fluid forms can relate as pieces of an interlocking jigsaw puzzle comprised of compatible plants, rather than predictable rows.

Landscapes are rarely level, inviting the designer to take full advantage of varying contours in the garden. Terraces, slopes, and gentle or radical grade changes can enhance the success of a layered design, offering optical illusions of depth and dimension, especially when taller plants accentuate the perspective.

There are many areas of a garden where layering conveys instant abundance. When plants have at least one characteristic in common—such as bloom time, flower shape, or stem color—they relate companionably. Even unusual pairings can speak a common language and wrap a garden in a glorious blanket of layers.

▶ A towering band of feather reed grass (*Calamagrostis* x *acutiflora* 'Karl Foerster') and a long planting of sedge (*Carex morrowii* 'Ice Dancer') accentuate the contours of a sloped border. The Masla greenhouse can be seen in the distance.

▲ Marj's bountiful bouquets give equal attention to humble annuals and the flowers of elegant shrubs. Arrangements, from left, include: 'Annabelle' hydrangea, monarda, zinnias, and black-eyed Susan (Rudbeckia fulgida 'Goldsturm'); and a purple-toned design featuring hydrangea, 'Autumn Joy' sedum, agapanthus, and globe thistle (*Echinops*).

On any given summer weekend, a loyal following of customers arrives at the Masla family's Fletcher Bay Flowers, selecting brilliant stems of lysimachia, dahlia, delphinium, and helianthus (sunflowers)—only $10 a bunch—on the honor system. The enterprise helps to grow the family's "vacation fund." "We have a following now, and as the season progresses, people like to see what's new," says Marj, a social worker.

Since buying their property in 1986, Nick and Marj have invested equal parts creativity and "sweat equity" to update their neglected 1940s farmhouse. They've added a deep, comfortable porch, erected a two-story addition and painted their house in tones of soft yellow with pale turquoise accents. The Maslas have installed a pond and waterfall, laid stone paths, and sliced three terraces into the gently sloping property. Where invasive vines once grew, they have planted a sunny cottage garden of eye-catching perennials, flowers that call to mind endless fields captured on the canvases of the Impressionists.

When Nick first planned the flower production beds, he planted row upon row of perennials. "My first priority was for the cutting garden; design was secondary," he confides. "But I don't mind the rows—

▲ The casually planned borders display depth and dimension, allowing the viewer to peer through tall stems and enjoy colorful glimpses of even more perennials. A planting of thick-stemmed agapanthus reveals hot pink monarda and 'Ember Glow' crocosmia planted beyond.

"My first priority was for the cutting garden; design was secondary."

▲ A rustic fence made from fir poles contains a primitive chair surrounded by berry-colored blooms, including cape fuchsia, ornamental oregano (*Origanum laevigatum* 'Hopley's Purple'), and the hybrid, *Lavatera thuringiaca* 'Barnsley'.
▶ Serving as an excellent vertical element in the Masla garden, narrow stems of purple loosestrife (*Lythrum virgatum*) are packed with magenta-purple clumps of blooms.

"But I don't mind the rows—because there's a layered effect even with straight lines."

because there's a layered effect even with straight lines. Long rows of delphiniums—with all those purples, light purples, and blues—make a great backdrop for other flowers."

Nick's linear sections have given way to mass plantings that fit together: plant forms intertwine and sections of compatible blooms seamlessly knit together. Depending on your vantage point, waves of stems topped with buttons, umbels, petals, and tassels give this garden a seemingly endless perspective. "The view from the driveway is my favorite—with all the layers," Nick observes. "Shapes take my eye from the sedums in the foreground to the eupatorium with its billowing pink flowers in the background—and the phlox flares up in the middle," he says, painting a floral portrait with his words.

Nick gleans ideas and inspiration from his friend Jay Fossett, who grew up in Maryland working with his father for the famed American landscape designers Wolfgang Oehme and James van Sweden. Nick credits Jay with introducing him to Oehme and van Sweden's prolific

use of perennials and grasses, replacing expansive lawns with dramatic elements of color, pattern, and structure. "I had three-foot-wide straight borders around the house, but Jay came over and said, 'You need to make these bigger and wider and more curved,' " Nick recalls.

He's since broken up generic foundation plantings, incorporating sinuous beds in front of the farmhouse. The circular edges and meandering lines are repeated in paths, borders and stone edging materials, a pleasing composition that draws the eye from one end of the garden to the other. "Color isn't the main thing—it's more about textures now," Nick says. "It's not wild, nor is it overcultivated." Large swaths of companionable plants help to define abundance for Nick. "I don't always plant with low-medium-high rules in mind. But I do combine similar flower heads, like hydrangeas with *Sedum* 'Autumn Joy'. When they're in bloom, it's like having dark purple clouds fill the garden."

When Nick plants a popular new grass like *Calamagrostis* x *acutiflora* 'Karl Foerster' (a bronze vertical sentinel in the landscape),

he uses it to shape graceful curving rows that draw visitors through the garden. "Grasses are so dynamic—they green out early and then shoot off. With 'Karl Foerster', I just got carried away—it's never just sitting there. Your eye goes boom-boom-boom—and you're led all the way into the distance."

Nick and Marj bring an artistic sentiment to everything they do in their environment. Marj fills glazed pots with elegant plantings, gracing the porches and patios with color and texture. Nick has hung vintage zinc-framed windows to enclose the greenhouse, commissioning a glass artist to design tiny panes with garden creatures where broken panes had to be replaced. If you look closely, you'll see a dragonfly, frog, and spider dancing across the windows.

Nick resourcefully salvages everything from plants to construction material for his garden. The sunny beds are edged in original Seattle cobblestone that was pulled from city streets during a municipal construction project. The twenty-foot-tall cedars, which help ▶ **50**

◀◀ The pale peach spires of the foxtail lily (*Eremurus*, hybrid cultivar) have an alluring, transparent quality.

◀ In the cottage garden, curved beds both structured and unstructured add layers that lure one deeper into the garden. A restrained palette relies on yellow loosestrife (*Lysimachia punctata*), the purple-blue blooms of catmint and lamb's ears (*Stachys byzantina*), green hostas, and burgundy foliage (*Lysimachia* 'Firecracker' and the distant Hollywood plum tree).

▲ The ethereal blooms of meadow rue (*Thalictrum aquilegifolium*) soften the appearance of adjacent plants.

Grasses are so dynamic—they green out early and then shoot off.

layering for abundance

View your garden as having many levels rather than as a two-dimensional canvas.

Creating an abundance of layers requires a multifaceted approach. View your garden as having many levels rather than as a two-dimensional canvas. Consider it from every angle—even from above and below—to determine how various areas can be connected or linked together. Use your own metaphor of shape, habit, or form.

It may be that you want to design intersecting crescents, which calls for a scheme with plants exhibiting a mounding habit or globe-shaped flowers to reinforce the idea. Or, devise an elongated *S*-shape with a starring perennial, shrub, or ornamental grass that snakes through a border, gathering up companion plants at its edges. Another possible inspiration might be to emulate the irregular rows of a dry-stack stone wall, achieved by staggering plants in alternating layers so that different forms visually move to the foreground as you meander past them.

Cues, Reference Points, and Inspiration: Reinforce the architecture of your home, as well as the character of your garden. An English-style garden may call for a formal hedge, typically seen as a monolithic row of evergreen shrubbery. If you instead take a layering approach to the hedge design, grow the classic hedgerow, planting a mixture of deciduous and evergreen shrubs and small trees, encouraging both fine needles and glossy leaves to intertwine. Tie the entire layer together by incorporating a variegated form of one of the primary shrubs, repeating it at least three times along the border.

Plant Pairings: Give yourself the challenge of combining two key plants and look for places where you can integrate them into the garden at important junctures, such as planted in two urns on the front porch or anchoring corners of a patio. Repeating these signature elements reinforces your design. It could be as simple as pairing two evergreen shrubs with winter interest—one beautiful combination is *Microbiota decussata* (carpet cypress) with *Ribes laurifolium* (a winter flowering currant). Evergreen sprays of the cypress take on a bronze tinge when temperatures drop, pairing attractively with early spring lime-colored racemes of the currant. And during the rest of the year, this pair contributes eye-catching foliage contrast.

Breaking Rules: Create open-form stem and branch structures that invite the viewer to peer through and see glimpses of denser plants beyond. Turn the rules upside down and place a row of taller agapanthus (African lily) in front of a vibrant, but shorter, bed of hot pink bee balm (*Monarda didyma*), red annual poppies (*Papaver somniferum*) and 'Ember Glow' crocosmias. The rounded clusters of bell-shaped, purple-blue agapanthus blossoms on thick stems, seem to float above the massed planting of lush salmon-pink perennial poppies, which are seen behind.

Similarly, you can use spires of taller plants to shoot up through a grouping of mid-range plants, acting as an exclamation point amidst an otherwise uniform paragraph of flowers. Other plants suggest a burst of fireworks exploding from a border. Achieve these looks with showy spikes of blue, purple, or white delphinium; narrow bottlebrush stalks of pink, purple, or red persicaria; the free-spirited white "gooseneck" flowers of *Lysimachia clethroides*; and the brilliant yellow, elongated flower heads of solidago (goldenrod).

▲ Shades of blue and green foliage move the eye from lady's mantle (*Alchemilla mollis*) in the foreground to taller plants at the back of the border, including hostas, *Ligularia stenocephala* 'The Rocket', and annual poppies.

▶ The rounded flower heads and mounded habit of *Sedum* 'Autumn Joy' reinforce the fluid lines of the curved front border. Providing explosions of vertical interest are plantings of feather reed grass (*Calamagrostis* x *acutiflora* 'Karl Foerster'), goldenrod (*Solidago rugosa* 'Fireworks'), and oxeye daisies (*Heliopsis helianthoides* var. *scabra* 'Summer Sun').

▲ The 10-by-20-foot greenhouse keeps a low profile in the middle of Nick's cutting garden. He fabricated the structure with materials old (recycled brick and windows) and new (corrugated and galvanized sheet metal).

"Now I'm trying to evolve into a shade gardener."

buffer street noise and lend a sylvan backdrop to the brilliant fields, were once three-foot saplings that Nick dug from drainage ditches. When he hears that nearby land will be clear-cut, Nick seeks permission to go in first and rescue native sword ferns. "Some of this has been kind of accidental," he acknowledges. "I like scrounging stuff."

As the trees grow, they have begun screening out the garden's sunnier areas, leading Nick to his newfound passion for shade gardening. He's removed some lower limbs of the taller evergreens to encourage dappled light into the shadows, and he's sought out

interesting shade plants to fill the understory. Several varieties of Japanese hydrangea, ligularia, ferns, rodgersia, hosta, pulmonaria, and epimedium now fill a large circular shade bed that encompasses the garden's wooded areas.

Happily, many of these plants are adding new blooms and interesting foliage to the cut garden repertoire. And Nick says they give him an excuse to experiment with yet another style of gardening. "You can always find something new to cut for arrangements, so now I'm trying to evolve into a shade gardener." ∼

Attention to details makes the utilitarian greenhouse an artful place, including a dragon kite that Nick and Marj found at a local folk festival, and tiny insect and bug windows made by local glass artist Julie Everett. A gargoyle figure stands sentry in the garden; the leaded-glass window offers a peek into the garden from the Masla kitchen.

abundance on a small scale

a tiny garden with big ideas

a tiny garden with big ideas

◄◄ **Several smaller areas of this charming garden are pieced together, quilt-like, by connecting tumbled bluestone pathways.**

▲ **Whether in sunshine or showers, Donna White *lives* outdoors, enjoying her landscape from the comfortable perch of a textile-covered daybed.**

By day, she is an accountant, albeit for a creative public relations agency. In her free time, Donna White is a prolific quilt designer whose sewing studio is packed from floor to ceiling with a rainbow of fabric swatches. Equally comfortable working with financial spreadsheets and oddly shaped bits of fabric, Donna demonstrates a gift for taking disparate pieces and synthesizing them into a harmonious finished product. Her approach to garden design in her 100-by-80-foot backyard reflects this left brain-right brain aptitude.

Abundance also
means having a fully
stocked pantry.

◄◄ The sheltered porch is a favorite
spot for family time and larger
gatherings.

▲ Nasturtiums, sweet peas, violets, and
trailing bacopa fill one of two cheery
window boxes that adorn the front of the
garden shed.

► Donna converted a standard "kit"
tool shed into a playful garden house,
painting the shingled structure with
vibrant shades of periwinkle, yellow, and
mint green. The aqua-colored metal roof
is topped with a weather vane.

Her intimate landscape reflects a similar design perspective, one in which utilitarian elements, such as a tool shed and a vegetable patch, are artfully rendered. She has linked small, cozy spaces that converse pleasingly with one another. Hallmarks of a spacious landscape—vistas, focal points, well-proportioned plantings, and a sense of enclosure—combine to give Donna's small backyard a feeling of abundance.

A mother of two college-age children, Donna comes from a background where "abundance" was equated with productive crop yields from the vegetable patch. "I grew up in a family of gardeners in Michigan where we never ate canned vegetables," she says, fondly recalling grandparents and parents who tended their organically grown gardens. "And even when we lived in metropolitan Detroit, my parents went to the country and bought their vegetables from farms."

Abundance also means having a fully stocked pantry, Donna maintains. And despite today's accessibility to organic produce in markets, she still prefers homegrown tomatoes, beets, squash, beans, pumpkins, and strawberries. ► **60**

at home in
the garden

A garden need not
be solitary for it to be
an intimate place.

Along with the cocooning of America, which in the language of home design means all things cozy and comforting, the garden has emerged as a metaphor for privacy, intimacy, and sanctuary. But for many who enjoy their landscapes, the idea of an intimate garden is best conveyed when the landscape is not merely private, but also welcoming and nurturing to its owner and others. A garden need not be solitary for it to be an intimate place.

The most intimate gardens shun a fortress approach, in which the world is kept at bay by thick hedges and locked gates. Gardens are indeed part of the larger landscape, as they connect us to the sky above, surrounding and distant scenery, the sounds and aromas of nature, or even the neighborhood's ambient noise. When a garden's interior spaces are thoughtfully balanced with these outside influences, it will feel private and removed, protecting us from our hectic schedules and everyday distractions.

Intimacy in an abundant garden relies on well-designed enclosures or partially secluded spaces, those that allow us to enjoy

being in the garden without feeling out in the open or exposed. Private spaces should also complement human proportions, simply achieved by stringing a hammock between two trees or placing a chaise and side table beneath a garden umbrella. There's nothing more romantically intimate than two chairs, side by side, placed where their occupants can enjoy the scenery together.

▲ ▲ The double-Adirondack bench adds a punch of color to Donna's garden—and invites her guests to sit and enjoy the scenery. The spot takes on added charm because Donna encourages self-sowing plants like this willowy mullein (*Verbascum* sp.).

▲ Nothing says "take a rest" more readily than a snooze-inducing hammock dressed with pillow and quilt.

Snug and secluded, enclosures can be created via planned spaces (courtyards, patios, porches, and seating nooks) or with plants (hedges, vines, a stand of trees, or a row of tall urns filled with a knockout combination of perennials). Bridging these two strategies are vertical structures, such as a trellis, arbor, columns, or even fabric panels suspended from a clothesline. Such features define the "walls" and "floors" of an enclosed space, but what about the "ceiling" above?

Any number of elements provides overhead shelter: a vine-covered arbor filters sunlight to grace the scenery below, a suspended canopy turns an exposed backyard into a cool retreat, or mood-setting twinkling lights decorate an impromptu party when strung from tree branches.

Physically and psychologically, our garden feels intimate when we treat it as an exclusive destination—away from the ordinary and mundane. Individual touches—a symbolic object, calming music, a lit candle, and a seat on which to rest—personalize the landscape. Combined, these elements give a garden the rare sense of intimacy—a soothing respite, a healing place, an inspiring experience in our own backyard.

▼ An open-grid design creates a half-wall around three sides of the porch, detailing that is repeated in the garden's other arbors and trellises.

The west-facing porch is a spacious extension into the garden of the kitchen and family room.

▲ An ornamental focal point of the knot garden is an oversized urn, planted with *Phygelius* x *rectus* 'Moonraker', one of Donna's favorite and oft-repeated garden perennials. The urn is surrounded by a symmetrical planting of golden barberry (*Berberis thunbergii* 'Aurea'), whose blooms echo the shed's yellow trim.

Donna's garden feels roomy in part because of a deeply covered porch that spans the twenty-foot width of her brick-and-wood-sided home. Added in 1997, the twelve-foot-deep, west-facing porch is a spacious extension into the garden of the kitchen and family room. At the center of the porch, four wide steps descend to the garden. An open-grid framework forms the lower walls, offering glimpses of blooms and foliage beyond.

"This makes the garden become part of the house," Donna points out. "It's the outdoor dining room. We read out there. If we have company, it's a nice place to hang out—everyone sits on the daybed, the steps, or in the wicker chairs." The porch takes on a Bohemian appearance ▶ **64**

◄ Clad in vines, the pergola-style arbor defines the terminus of the backyard and helps to screen the landscape for privacy. Donna has further separated the garden by elevating her borders with a low retaining wall on either side of a short staircase.

◄◄ A potting bench and ample shelving are practical touches in the ornamental garden shed.

▲ Clockwise, from top: Tools of the trade include pots, a pitcher, and watering can; a botanical plaque hangs from the kitchen garden's arbor; *Rosie* drinks from a decorative birdbath; and a collection of colorful glass is ready for Donna's next mosaic project.

▲ This alluring display of blooms and berries represents the warm side of the color wheel, with golden spikes of *Lysimachia punctata*, red-berried hypericum, and soft yellow yarrow (*Achillea millefolium*). A luminous glass finial accents the equally dazzling plants.

thanks to a handy pile of Donna's patterned quilts, ready for people to grab on chilly evenings. Brilliantly printed and pieced, the textiles reflect Donna's penchant for contemporary designs and her comfort living among an array of bright hues—and they repeat the pinks, yellows, reds, and purples of the garden's palette.

"When I quilt, I use lots of color, a lot of different fabrics—and I don't tend to use traditional patterns," she says. "Where a quilt pattern might call for four fabrics, I use fifty different ones."

Applied to a garden, some would argue this design approach is too busy. Donna disagrees. "To me, the least interesting gardens are those limited to tidy little rows of annuals. I like lots of different flowers to move your eye around the garden, just as when viewing different colors in a quilt—I use a lot of the same principles."

A year after adding the porch, the property's septic system required replacement, which meant ripping out large portions of the back lawn. After the bulldozers left, Donna faced a blank slate—and an opportunity to redesign her garden. Her children were growing up, which meant she could say goodbye to the sandbox and tree house. Of two minds—the farmer's daughter and the textile artist—Donna pieced together ideas for pairing a prolific vegetable patch with lavish mixed borders.

She considered the new landscape from the vantage point of her open-air porch, which overlooks the garden on three sides and is connected to the house via a pair of French doors and a bank of windows. "I love looking at the garden from above," she notes. With the feeling of an elevated loft, the porch allows Donna to survey the garden, enjoying the perspective offered by informal and formal areas linked by pathways, low fencing, vine-clad trellises, and clipped hedges.

From her sketches for the new garden, Donna used bluestone pavers to install a walkway that connects each of the visually stimulating areas. She created an informal knot garden just beyond the steps, placing a perennial-filled urn at its center and clipped boxwood balls in each corner. The scene provides an artful focal point around which the rest of the garden is designed.

To the right, an outside patio and kitchen garden are contained by a picket fence and entered via a cheery arbor-topped gate. Donna devised unique framing for her raised vegetable beds. She imbedded fragments of colored glass, Japanese glass floats, and found objects (including countless golf balls that have landed here from the adjacent fairway) into wet concrete to form a mosaic-like decorative pattern in the finished frames. "The kitchen garden itself is very quilt-like," she explains, pointing out its patchwork appearance, created by intermingling herbs, salad greens, and annuals that don't adhere to tidy rows. "I just can't let anything be perfectly square."

To the left stands a brilliantly painted tool shed, finished in shades of periwinkle, yellow, and mint green and sheltered with a coordinating hip roof in aqua-colored metal. Double barn doors swing open on the side to accommodate the lawnmower. Annuals spill out of a pair of window boxes mounted on either side of a Dutch-style front door. Clipped boxwood balls and soft perennials lend a cottage-style feeling to the entry garden. ▶ **68**

The kitchen garden itself is very quilt-like, created by intermingling herbs, salad greens, and annuals that don't adhere to tidy rows.

▼ **Bright red with yellow centers, these hybrid daylilies borrow the brilliant palette of Donna's quilting designs.**

designing
intimate spaces

Create intentional areas

that invite daydreaming,

reading poetry, or

listening to music.

In the midst of designing, planting, and tending to an abundant garden, one that overflows with a profusion of blooms, plan for the moments when all you want to do is pause, rest, and just enjoy the garden. Those are the times when intimate places are most needed and appreciated. There is a joy that comes with just *being,* rather than always digging, weeding, and watering. Give yourself one or more spots in the garden for such intimate pleasures as absorbing the beauty around you, admiring the surroundings, and experiencing solitude or the company of others. Create intentional areas that invite daydreaming, reading poetry, or listening to music. Make the garden worthy of the laziest day.

Here are some ideas, borrowed from many of the garden makers in *The Abundant Garden.*

Use Transparent or Translucent Screening: Solid gates, dense hedges, and thickly planted perimeters can easily impose their forbidding moods on a landscape.

When you interrupt the constant plane of a wood fence by inserting occasional panels of latticework, you'll be rewarded with increased light flowing into the garden. Openings also support carefree tendrils and stems of climbing vines. Similarly, you can selectively prune some of the lower and mid-height branches in trees or shrubs, creating niches and gaps for light and views (consult a certified arborist for help with this task). The presence of deciduous trees offers yet another transparent element to the landscape. During the warmer months when you're frequently outdoors, a deciduous shade tree also provides a cool canopy of shelter. Yet by late autumn, when the leaves fall, you will appreciate instead the warmth and light ushered into the garden by the tree's bare branches.

Change the Grade for Emphasis: A sunken garden is a design solution for intimacy, especially if your landscape is highly public. When you lower the grade and allow a portion of the garden to descend by six to eighteen inches, you create the illusion of secrecy and privacy for anyone who visits. Excavation can be expensive, however, so if

you can't afford to dig out an area, use components of a sunken garden to suggest one. Narrow the entrance to the space, which implies that it has an anteroom leading into an intimate, interior room. Erect a low wall around a patio or courtyard to define and contain the area. Keep seating close to the ground, using cushioned furnishings for a relaxed mood.

Celebrate the Senses: One of the strongest, memory-inducing senses is that of smell. What better way to celebrate our

▲ Chimes bring a gentle melody into the garden. They hang from a bracket that's partially obscured by the blooms of a pink Japanese snowbell tree (*Styrax japonicus* 'Pink Chimes').

▶ Donna's kitchen garden can be entered through either of two arbor-topped gates. The overhead arbors offer yet another surface on which artwork can be hung and vines can be trained. The left arbor displays the enormous blooms of white-flowering clematis; the right arbor supports golden hops (*Humulus lupulus* 'Aureus') and *Rosa* 'Eden Climber', a pale pink variety.

favorite fragrances of childhood, romance, and nostalgic memories than by infusing our garden with sweet-smelling plants? From winter daphne and witch hazel to an unforgettable bouquet of summer sweet peas, we are instinctively attracted to the garden's most aromatic places. Give your garden a tactile quality by adding masses of soft, fuzzy, or feathery plants to the places where your ankles or hands will brush against them. Touching the velvety leaves of lamb's ears or rubbing our faces in an intoxicating bed of herbs triggers any number of emotions—most likely pleasurable. We can add a secret music to the garden through the song of water or the tinkle of melodic chimes. Highly personal, these sensory ingredients in the garden add up to an intimate sanctuary—one to which we immediately turn for refreshment after a long, busy day away from the garden.

▲ From top: A stone orb punctuates a corner planting of grassy sedge (*Carex* sp.) and hardy geraniums; golf balls are "found objects" that Donna has imbedded into homemade concrete beds in the kitchen garden; and glass pieces form a mosaic stepping stone.

The knot garden's symmetrical proportions give way to a circular strolling lawn and its rounded form. Much as when a quilt's piecework moves from a tightly controlled central motif into a border stitched with loose shapes, Donna's square-knot garden transitions nicely into curved outlines, expressed in twin crescent-shaped mixed borders that mirror each other. Two planter boxes with conifer-ball topiaries flank the opening through which one moves from path to lawn.

Plants selected for their attractive foliage, branch structure, and floral beauty thrive on either side of the lawn. Numerous hydrangeas lend their glossy leaves and long-blooming mop heads, interspersed among a crazy quilt of golden carex, fragrant winter hazel (*Corylopsis* spp.), ghost bramble (*Rubus biflorus*), rodgersia, hypericum, purple-leafed ninebark (*Physocarpus opulifolius* 'Diabolo'), a weeping katsura (*Cercidiphyllum japonicum* f. *pendulum*), golden chain tree (*Laburnum anagyroides*), miscanthus grasses, and roses.

Privacy was a major issue for Donna, who wanted to enjoy her landscape without having to come face-to-face with golfers, stray balls, and misguided golf carts prone to running over the perennials. "I worked hard to achieve privacy from the golf course," she notes. "I wanted seclusion, because otherwise, I felt like I had two front yards."

She commissioned Ed Buckley, a local woodworker, to build a pergola-style arbor that serves as the garden's back entrance and provides informal screening. A succession of blooming vines, including honeysuckle, clematis, and *Rosa banksiae*, a climber, creeps over and through the lattice sides and peaked roof of the structure. At the garden's edge, a bluestone-faced concrete retaining wall elevates the landscape so it is above the view of ever-present golfers.

For Donna, the landscape is highly personal, an expression of her creativity and warm personality. "My favorite moments here are when people sit on my back porch, wrapped in quilts, snuggling on the daybed, and spending time together." ◠

◄ **Resembling an enchanted portal, the pergola-style arbor makes this garden seem more secluded, especially when the pale pink *Clematis montana* vine is in full bloom.**

▼ **Intense fuchsia shades blend with saturated golden hues to fill one of two crescent-shaped perennial and shrub borders that edge the circular lawn.**

"My favorite moments here are when people sit on my back porch, wrapped in quilts, spending time together."

horticulture heaven

a plant collector's garden

a plant collector's garden

◄◄ In Carol's bowl garden, beardless irises and candelabra primulas stand jewel-like against a spectrum of green. A full-moon maple (*Acer shirasawanum* 'Aureum') glows to the right.

▲ A profusion of hydrangeas and an eye-catching golden boxleaf honeysuckle (*Lonicera nitida* 'Baggesen's Gold') surround the Nantucket-style house.

arol Johanson has elevated the status of her gardenworthy plants, valuing her collection as others might regard a group of fine oil paintings. She is both curator and caretaker of a well-edited landscape—one that welcomes a diverse selection of plants that thrive in conditions ranging from full shade to western exposure.

The first hint that you're arriving at a place where plants are held in high esteem begins at the entrance to the Johanson driveway. A glorious stand of golden locust trees heralds the journey to come. The scene conveys dynamic energy, not just from the staggered placement of the elegant trees or the sound of breezes tickling the oval leaflets, but from the sense of movement suggested by a ribbon of smooth black rocks flowing river-like beneath them.

▲ From every level of the tiered property and house, the panorama is captured.

As the 180-foot-long drive descends, it's impossible to anticipate what's hidden around the corner. "I thought it would be cool if you couldn't see the house until you came around the bend," Carol enthuses. Along the left side of the driveway, opposite the dry riverbed and golden trees, stands a Japanese-style lantern crafted by Karin Corbin, a local artist. The piece provides an architectural reference to the Johanson garden's subtle Pacific Rim influences and illuminates a dense screen of pines, Douglas firs, and deodar cedars. The conifers give way to a massed planting of finely textured rock rose shrubs (*Cistus* sp.), tall enough to prevent you from peeking over them to see what's next.

Just beyond, where the driveway bends, two equally dazzling tableaux come into focus. Like seeing a highly detailed impression through a telephoto lens, the first scene appears directly ahead: Rendered in warm shades of burgundy and gold, a border of fluid grasses and statuesque perennials reveals a small opening at its edge, inviting you to step through to a secluded garden. ▶ **78**

▲ A café-like setting beneath the arbor offers a sheltered place from which to enjoy the diverse plant collections that envelop this scene. Carol displays her potted specimens on an antique French wire plant stand.

◄ A Japanese lantern gives visual pleasure to this humble scene of stone and pine.

discovering and making the most of views

Highlight the best of your garden.

Both plantings and structures are integral to scene-setting techniques that enhance our visual enjoyment of landscapes. To make the most of its vistas and views, highlight the best of your garden—whether you are showcasing outward views that allow you to gaze on enthralling distant scenes or interior views that draw attention to thoughtfully arranged displays of plants, water features, or sculpture.

Chances are your garden offers an amazing array of views; but are you taking advantage of them? What is the first thing you notice when looking outward from your home, through a doorway or window? What are your garden's focal points?

With some planning, you can accentuate your landscape's best views, highlighting its vistas and framing charming focal points. A pleasing *view* offers an area of your landscape to be seen—it commands attention when framed by ornamental trees, arbors, or trellises. A pleasing *vista* is usually savored from a distance, allowing you to borrow nature's beauty as a backdrop for your own garden. Be it a grouping of ornamental trees

or a fountain, a *focal point* is often displayed at the heart of a garden, lending a sense of drama or calming balance to a design.

When there is no natural view to appreciate, you can devise your own. Even in the tiniest of gardens, it's possible to create

and highlight a scene. Position a grouping of container plantings just outside a picture window to be observed as a botanical still life on a winter day. Begin by selecting noteworthy areas you naturally see while walking through the garden. Or, gaze outward from a terrace or patio, toward the perimeter of the garden. Does a fence, a hedge, or the side of a neighbor's garage fill the scene? Once you're aware of the potential vistas, consider opening up the best ones or downplaying or transforming unwanted ones.

Garden designers use visual tricks to draw and direct the eye—and you can adopt these strategies in your own backyard. Highlight your garden's best views by creating a sense of movement and energy, perhaps with ornamental grasses or an overhead arbor clad in vines, allowing the delightful destination beyond to be perceived as a dramatic extension of the garden's visual reach. Employ techniques that frame and define unforgettable views: An opening in a dense hedge ignites curiosity to discover what's inside. Color is another attention-grabbing device. Use it to turn ordinary walls, gates, and garden furniture into dramatic elements that focus attention or unify a scene. Garden lighting increases the garden's magnetism, especially when used to create spectral effects on a moonless night.

Select plants, place stepping-stones, or erect garden structures to make the most of

▲ ▲ Carol collaborated with architect-designer Seri Yeckel to create the Japanese gate in her serenity garden.

▲ Carol relies on her containers as a laboratory for observing how new plants perform in her garden's microclimate.

a would-be view. Edge a patio with pots of dwarf conifers to lend it prominence. Add a strolling path that leads to a half-hidden but alluring area of the garden. Even if the focal point you want to magnify is in a small or narrow spot, planting a tree or placing a statue so that it lines up perfectly with the gate that leads there will endow it with a bold dimension. You've instantly created a view in a once unnoticed corner of the garden.

Discover the many vantage points in your home and garden. Once you observe nature's lovely vistas, think about how you might refine and heighten their impact. With thoughtful planning and placement of plants, furniture, structures, and artifacts, you can turn an ordinary view into a spectacular visual treat.

▼ This outdoor sitting area is adjacent to the serenity garden. Partially enclosed by a stone retaining wall, it feels like a sunken garden.

This landscape is
more than an
encyclopedia of
interesting trees and
unusual shrubs,
perennials, and vines.

▼ The stone retaining wall not only
helps terrace the steep property, it
creates a functional rockery for planting
drought-tolerant and Mediterranean
plants, including rosemary, lavender,
and euphorbia.

Suddenly, a breathtaking vista appears, offering a wide-angle view of the Johanson property: one-and-one-half acres of cultivated borders that resemble a private botanical garden and that enfold a Nantucket-style house. A 120-foot-long retaining wall along the home's west side forms a shoulder-high terrace level; drought-tolerant Mediterranean plants in sunset hues grow above the stonework and among its open spaces. The edge of the property's cultivated areas is well defined by a flowing border of ornamental grasses, which reveals views of the expansive waterfront below.

Lovingly created and cared for by Carol, an ardent plant enthusiast, this landscape is more than an encyclopedia of interesting trees and unusual shrubs, perennials, and vines. While she has chosen specimens for their rare appeal or unique bloom, bark, or foliage characteristics, she's thoughtfully placed each with attention to the garden's overall appearance. As a result, the landscape is a pleasing and profuse

▲ Perennials like this scarlet
wallflower (*Erysimum* sp.) and
sun-loving herbs occupy the
planting pockets between
chunks of basalt that form the
west-facing retaining wall.

portrait that thrives on several levels: plants stair-step toward the nearby waterfront, follow curving brick pathways, cascade over stone retaining walls, and border a small gem of a shed.

"My goal is to have a garden that works in a particular spot, with the right combinations for seasonal interest, color, and texture," says Carol.

Carol's pursuit of unusual plants is equal only to her desire to cultivate nearly every inch of land once populated by alder saplings, blackberry vines, and rotting cedars. "The property was very wet—water drained through the land from the south and the east," she recounts. "But we tried to work with the contours of this land."

Carol and her husband Gene Johanson have invested more than fifteen years in developing their house and gardens, which overlook Port Orchard Sound off Bainbridge Island's western shore. The couple moved here in 1988, purchasing the property from a nonprofit organization that had received it as part of a benefactor's estate. Undeveloped, the land sloped steeply to the water's edge, where a ramshackle beach cottage was once the only structure on the lot. "When we found this property, we had to hike in to see it," Carol recalls. "We came down the path and

Plants stair-step
toward the nearby
waterfront, follow
curving brick
pathways, cascade
over stone retaining
walls, and border a
small gem of a shed.

▲ From top: A dainty crown from the candelabra primula; a blue-crested iris with streaks of yellow; purple-rose *Tradescantia* x *andersoniana*.

▶▲ Petal-like bracts atop the blooms of Spanish lavender (*Lavandula stoechas* subsp. *pedunculata*) sparkle in the mixed border.

▶ This border of phlox, Russian sage, and annual snapdragons partially hides the garden shed.

▶▼ The pure blue racemes of *Parahebe perfoliata*.

discovered raw land with a marginal road running through it. But this is the property we really loved."

During the challenging three-year construction project, Carol, Gene, and their young son, Colin (now twenty-four), lived in the 750-square-foot cabin, which they'd remodeled to make it habitable. Living there gave Carol a daily opportunity to study the areas where she would later design her glorious gardens.

"We would come up and walk the property; we had a stepladder and we'd move it around with us. For example, we looked for where the sun came across the property, which gave us an idea of where we would put the kitchen—because I've always loved the eastern sun," she explains. Working with Bob Hobble, a local island architect, the

Johansons built a two-story grey-shingled house, distinguished by large, view-capturing windows, perky green-and-white awnings, and generously proportioned outdoor decks, terraces, and patios.

In both the house and garden, Carol and Gene have found ways to capitalize on the stunning distant views of sea and mountains. They have tucked seating in unexpected corners of the garden, out-of-the-way places from which the usually subtle, sometimes dramatic movements of sky and water can be observed. The couple has also enhanced garden viewing from several interior perspectives, devising scenes that can be admired through an open window or framed by the arbor-covered patio. "We wanted to be able to walk outside every room on the main level to access the garden," Carol says.

"The names of these gardens often come to me before the gardens come to me."

Most of the initial budget earmarked for landscaping was gobbled up by the need to correct drainage problems and to construct more than 600 linear feet of retaining wall from basalt boulders. Consequently, by the time she turned to planting design, Carol had to take a more affordable, hands-on approach. She enlisted the help of Terri Stanley, a Bainbridge Island designer and horticulturist, who introduced Carol to a plant-centered design process.

The partnership triggered in Carol a passion for horticultural specimens both rare and hard to find. "Our collaboration was very valuable for me," Carol recalls of the few years during which she worked with Terri. The women sketched out some of the landscape's first planting beds and brick-covered walk, shopped for choice

▼ A streak of burgundy-rose barberry (*Berberis thunbergii*), planted en masse, makes a brilliant statement at the edge of the bowl garden. A touch of contrast is found in the form of golden spirea (*Spiraea japonica* 'Goldflame').

specimens, and decided how to group them in the garden. "I really view Terri as my mentor," Carol adds. Like an enthusiastic protégé, Carol has continued to experiment with her own ideas on the garden, editing some areas and adding to others. "It's a full-time job scouting for plants," she deadpans.

While cultivating various areas of her multileveled garden, Carol intuitively named many of them. By labeling unique areas in the garden, Carol says she's being both practical and poetic: "I'll say 'I'm up in the triangle bed,' so Gene knows where to find me." Areas are distinguished by Carol's attention to individual plant choices and the role they play together in creating the garden's mood. "The names of these gardens often come to me before the gardens come to me," she says.

Carol envisioned having a "serenity garden," which led to an Asian-themed viewpoint in her landscape's southwest corner. ▶ **86**

▲ In its earlier existence, this humble structure served as a storage shed and a doghouse. Now, Carol has dressed it up with French doors, crank-windows, comfortable wicker seating, and shelves that hold much-used reference books. •

framing
for effect

Think of each plane as you direct the viewer's eye toward nearby and distant scenes.

Good photographers learn how to crop the extraneous details from the outer edges of a picture to improve its quality. Similarly, you can improve the overall picture of your garden when you impose a "frame" around its views. The classic elements of design, such as line, shape, texture, and color, are useful tools when composing and editing the desired scene. Simplicity is a key concept to keep in mind. Strive for an uncomplicated selection of plants, a cohesive bloom and foliage palette, and garden structures that relate sensibly to your house's architecture.

The frame through which you consider and enjoy a view may have vertical components—defined by doorways, tall plants, or an opening in the fence. Arches

and arbors above or pathways and stepping-stones below form the horizontal components. Think of each plane as an important piece of the overall picture as you direct the viewer's eye toward nearby and distant scenes.

Carol and Gene Johanson have played up their garden's best features by enhancing the natural views and vistas seen from their

property on Bainbridge Island. They've intentionally devised places within and adjacent to their house and throughout the garden from which to see breathtaking views. Equally important, these gardenmakers have used artwork, architecture, and furniture to design scenes within the garden that can be viewed and appreciated up close.

Here are some of the tricks and techniques you can employ to frame views and highlight scenes.

Enhance Sightlines: As your eye travels through a window or doorway into the garden, follow the direct axis. Where does your gaze rest? Emphasize the importance of that perspective by displaying an urn filled with perennials or a small sculpture on a pedestal. Or, plant a flowering tree that will create a glorious scene as it matures.

Balance the Composition: Frame a view that's near or distant with symmetrical plantings, such as a pair of columnar conifers that will indicate the opening to a garden

▲ The waterfall's descent draws the eye outward, through an opening in the trees, to see the elevated deck and the view beyond.

▶ A stone slab offers a place of serenity to observe the garden's interior or outward-facing views.

path. Or suggest asymmetrical balance by offsetting a large tree on one side of the view with a grouping of garden furniture on the other.

Open up Views: A day of garden cleanup may be the best way to improve your vistas. Overgrown shrubs and crowded plantings can be thinned to make room for a glimpse of distant scenes. Instead of cutting down a large tree that obstructs your view, invest in the expertise of a certified arborist who can open up "view zones" with targeted

branch removal, allowing you to enjoy both the tree and the view beyond.

Go Diagonal: One designer trick, especially useful in small gardens, is to enhance diagonal sightlines with pathways and plantings placed at a 45-degree angle to your house. This method allows you to see extended views through the garden, while giving the illusion of larger space.

Highlight Nature: When you plant an eye-catching "island" on the sunrise or sunset side of your house, take advantage of

how the sun can act as a backlight for a plant's foliage color or overall form. Choose trees and shrubs with golden or scarlet foliage so you can appreciate the glowing beauty of horizontal light at dawn or dusk.

▲ The deeply cut, laced foliage and rounded form of the golden elderberry (*Sambucus* sp.) dominate the foreground of this scene. The shrub border hides a pathway to the garden shed and the secret garden.

▲ Twisted leaves distinguish this
unusual willow, planted along the
edge of Carol's bowl garden.

► Ferns and other moisture-loving
plants edge the waterfall.

The intriguing destination is reached by taking a softly cushioned journey through the wooded edges of the Johanson property, over the threshold of a handcrafted Japanese gate, and past a custom-forged wisteria arbor. The quiet excursion culminates at Carol's serenity garden, where a cascading waterfall spills over rocks into a calm pool at its base. Guests enjoy this naturalistic scene from an elevated deck, perfect for outdoor gatherings.

Another secluded viewing deck is called the "secret garden." Obscured from view behind an exuberant border of tall grasses and pink-flowered *Lavatera* 'Barnsley', this circular deck offers Carol and Gene a welcoming respite on hot days. They relax in a pair of Adirondack chairs and enjoy peekaboo sights of shipping and sailing activity on the waters below.

In the "triangle garden," Carol relies on tall perennials and ornamental trees to softly enclose a three-sided carpet of lawn that juts out above the driveway. "This is the perfect lookout," she says, gesturing to the comfortable bench, just large enough for two to sit. Since this is one of the property's highest vantage points, it offers panoramic views of the rest of the garden. Season after season, golden elderberry (*Sambucus nigra* 'Aurea'), wine-tinged astrantia (*Astrantia major*), salmon-flowered cape fuchsia (*Phygelius* x *rectus*), coppery feather reed grass (*Calamagrostis* x *acutiflora* 'Karl Foerster'), and silvery maiden grass (*Miscanthus sinensis* 'Gracillimus') give this area's "living wall" a tactile quality.

In designing this area, Carol has taken advantage of its somewhat protected conditions to grow several unique specimen trees, including the Japanese stewartia (*Stewartia pseudocamellia*), which will display peeling pink-brown bark as it matures, and katsura tree (*Cercidiphyllum japonicum*), appreciated for its golden-orange fall color and burnt-sugar fragrance. There's also a rarely seen franklinia (*Franklinia alatamaha*), with fragrant, cup-shaped white flowers, and a Japanese umbrella pine (*Sciadopitys verticillata*), which is characterized by glossy needles that whorl around each branch.

The "triangle garden" leads to yet more borders, continuing the palette with touches of hot oranges and sultry pinks. Late summer dahlias rise above the zigzagged leaves of honey bush (*Melianthus major*) and the upright spikes of a massed planting of knotweed (*Persicaria* sp.). Lantern-style lilies and the spherical blooms of 'Annabelle' hydrangeas dance in concert against the plum-green clouds of Japanese cedar (*Cryptomeria japonica* 'Elegans').

A large, oval strolling lawn leads to Carol and Gene's front door and serves as an inviting entrance to the gardens beyond. Called the "bowl garden" because it rests at the base of the landscape's upper slope, the area is screened by conifers lining the driveway. Since the planting beds here are partially hidden from sunlight, they provide Carol a laboratory for experimenting with novel shade-loving plants. The overall palette here is green-on-green, which brings to the forefront each plant's unique shape or form. Among her favorites are epimedium, hosta, mahonia, pulmonaria, hellebore, vancouveria, sarcococca, rodgersia, and ferns like *Blechnum spicant* and *Polystichum munitum*.

When asked to speculate on the mind-boggling quantity of plants she grows here, Carol graciously avoids the question, saying she doesn't keep count since the number constantly changes. "There's something exciting about finding the unique and the unusual plant, but I also liké growing common plants that can be used in different ways for delightful results." ∽

The overall palette here is green-on-green, which brings to the forefront each plant's unique shape or form.

▲ To enjoy their own version of "horticulture heaven," Carol and Gene often retire to this pair of chaises.

cherished place

a romantic golden garden

a romantic golden garden

If there is one word that describes Caren and David Anderson's garden, it's *verdant.* From towering evergreens that edge the garden to the calming presence of a small lawn, green in every shade and form gives this two-acre Northwest landscape an inviting tranquility. It serves as the canvas against which Caren has planted artful compositions of foliage and flower alike. She has a seemingly effortless approach to design, which results in inventive pairings of ordinary and rare plants, such as a cluster of unusual Japanese barberry shrubs (*Berberis thunbergii* 'Helmond Pillar') that emerge like red-burgundy columns from golden tufts of Japanese forest grass (*Hakonechloa macra* 'Aureola') that carpets the ground below.

◄◄ In the secret garden, woodland plants such as ferns and hostas are warmed by the dazzling citrus-colored springtime tulips and a carpet of golden creeping Jenny (*Lysimachia nummularia* 'Aurea') that spills onto the mulched pathway.

▲ Colored by terra-cotta pigment, an organic sculpture, commissioned from island artists David Lewis and George Little, emerges from the mixed perennial border as a graphic focal point.

"Almost all of my quilts had a garden focus."

◄ Garden seating provides a vantage point for the expansive view of the garden, overlooking the rose arbor on the lower terrace.

▲ An old shed overlooking the pond and lower garden was ideally situated for Caren's studio. She recruited her parents to help convert the rugged structure into a cozy refuge where she can come inside from the garden to draw and paint. A Japanese wisteria softens the roofline, while shade plants grow beneath the cedars.

In the late 1970s, after living in Oregon, the Andersons moved to Bainbridge Island, Washington. They discovered an early twentieth-century cottage situated on a two-acre terraced lot, with enticing views of Puget Sound beyond. A textile artist whose work includes contemporary wall quilts, Caren initially focused her design efforts on her home and interiors. "I'd always liked having a nice yard, but it wasn't really my passion," she confides.

As Caren and David began to cultivate their property, the common thread between textile art and garden design emerged. "You know how things evolve and you don't even know?" Caren muses. "Almost all of my quilts had a garden focus—landscape imagery, floral gardens, atmospheres like clouds, and different outdoor scenes—but always the garden."

Having worked with wonderful fabrics, it's no surprise that Caren loves highly tactile plants. "I'm a texture person—that's what I'm most drawn to—foliage color and texture," Caren points out. "I started out not liking flowers. I just wanted evergreens and the woodland feeling."

Yet like piecing together a quilt that requires interesting contrasts in prints and hues, Caren soon discovered an important role for blooms in her garden. "I started adding color and texture with plants that have interesting foliage and blooms that last longer throughout the year."

In the early 1990s, Caren began collaborating with garden designer and horticulturist Terri Stanley of Mesogeo Nursery on Bainbridge Island. "Terri introduced me to things most gardeners weren't doing and plants most nurseries didn't even have," Caren says. "I knew exactly what I wanted to do—I had the concept—but I didn't have the knowledge ▶ **98**

▲ Paved in bluestone and edged by weathered brick, the side entrance to the house serves as an intimate courtyard. Other than the profusion of hydrangea blooms, Caren restricted her choices here to ferns, heucheras, and other foliage-interest shade plants.

"I'm a texture person—that's what I'm most drawn to—foliage color and texture."

ornamentation for artful living

Place ornaments with a dose of restraint.

As the lines between interior design and exterior design are blurred, we comfortably travel in and out of the garden. We bring the best of our landscapes indoors on a year-round basis, whether that means forcing branches to flower in late winter arrangements or lining our windowsills with fresh herbs. Likewise, we extend home comforts outdoors, moving to garden "rooms" for peaceful pursuits or designing expansive patios to accommodate warm fireplaces or *al fresco* dinners with friends.

For those with "a garden lifestyle," the use of furniture and ornamentation has added importance, allowing us to appreciate everything from unusual artwork to flea market finds, while enjoying them in relation to our plants. We paint a scene, compose a vignette, or establish a gallery-like feeling when we display precious objects side by side with foliage and flower—or better yet, partially hidden among the stems and branches of a favorite plant.

Drawing on tenets of interior design, it's important to furnish and adorn a garden with a sense of proportion and scale in mind. Where and how we add objects implies the value we give them. Outdoors, the scale with

which we work is seemingly endless, as the sky above is indeed vaster than the limitations presented by a home's nine-foot-high ceilings. Whether it's a piece of sculpture, a duet of comfortable chaises, an architectural fragment or a memento from a trip abroad, ornamentation must be substantial enough to stand up to the spaciousness of a garden and the dimensions of a home's porch, patio or terrace.

Artwork in the garden should be highly personal. Its placement can fall anywhere on a continuum that ranges between playfulness and restraint. Some gardeners take a curatorial approach to their ornamentation, isolating a cherished bronze from a clutter of plants. Others prefer the organic approach of letting objects and plants happily commingle. But place ornaments with a dose of restraint: too many charming figures or decorative trinkets result in a cluttered, distracting design.

Ornamentation is a fitting element of an abundant garden when it fits into the landscape with relevance. Perhaps a rectangular lawn seems ordinary—until you've placed at its center a pedestal holding a shallow bowl of water to reflect the sky. The long green hedge is functional, but when a colorful bench, flanked by two graceful trees, is added to the foreground, the hedge becomes backdrop to an inviting tableau. And when a relatively horizontal collection of perennials needs pizzazz, that's when a vertical piece—a trellis or painted column—adds a certain punch to the design (and an opportunity to add a graceful climber or two).

Perhaps more important than anything else, the nonplant pieces you incorporate into the garden should be a reflection of you and your personal style.

▲ A silvery blue spruce and fuzzy lamb's ears provide a cool layer of textures; below these plants is a lush green carpet of baby's tears. Orange crocosmia and bright pink fuchsia blooms dance above the foliage. The English chimney pipe is a favorite architectural element in the garden.

"I wanted plants with something else to offer than their blooms—plants with multiple interest."

◄◄ At the heart of the Anderson garden is a lavish pond. Landscaped with an array of tropical plants, the setting is an alluring summertime destination.

◄ Clockwise, from top left: Mouths open, koi fishes await their next meal; blooms to tantalize the senses include a robust pink rose, a sky blue Himalayan poppy (*Meconopsis betonicifolia*), mauve-colored clematis in full bloom, and a dew-kissed cluster of English roses; sedums and succulents fill in the crags and cracks of a rockery in the herb garden.

of plants. Terri had an encyclopedia of plants in her head, and she knew what was going to do well in what condition, plus she knew about foliage color, sizes, and blooms."

While much has changed since Caren and Terri first began creating the Anderson garden, Caren credits the designer with educating her about an amazing diversity of plants and ways to use them in the garden. "I was drawn to Terri because of her incredible knowledge of foliage plants," Caren says. "When I first started working with her, not very many people were talking about using golden, silver, or red foliage colors. But I wanted plants with something else to offer than their blooms—plants with multiple interest."

As an artist would embroider a quilt with touches of brilliant color, Caren has added foliage-strong perennials, climbing roses, colorful clematis vines, and ornamental shrubs to her garden repertoire. But hers is not a collector's garden with one type of every plant. Restraint

is the theme of this landscape. Where other backyards seem filled to overflowing, Caren has brought a level of elegance and sophistication to her garden.

"Restraint is the best thing for me," she acknowledges. "When it comes right down to it, I'm always happier when it's simpler. There are some plants that run throughout my whole garden—ferns, heucheras, hostas, and hardy fuchsias—and I used to think I should be able to come up with more plants. But then I realized my garden has a unity because of these plants."

To illustrate the importance of her "less is more" philosophy, Caren singles out the four-post rose arbor. She has planted the fragrant pink climber *Rosa* 'Constance Spry' at the base of each, training the English

◄ Caren plants herbs and salad greens in front of the three-foot tall concrete foundation, which also serves as the wall against which two apple trees have been trained into espaliered forms.

▲ A Paris flea market find, the verdigris-finished copper roof vent complements this composition of rhododendrons, hostas, and Solomon's seal.

Restraint is

the theme of

this landscape.

▲ Heucheras, hostas, and astilbes compose a blissfully soft edge to the design of this oval-shaped island.

"When the roses
are blooming, that
arbor is the center
of the garden."

roses to engulf the top of the arbor. "When the roses are blooming, that arbor is the center of the garden. Your eye can rest there and it's tranquil," Caren says.

She varies the show at eye level, however, removing the rose foliage along the post to make room for four varieties of clematis. "The clematis vines wrap around the rose trunks and bloom at different times—you can stick your nose right in them," she proclaims.

Elsewhere, Caren has trained a Japanese lavender-hued wisteria to clamber up and over the top of her cozy studio, a welcoming artist's oasis in the middle of the garden. Once a chicken coop or storage shed, the twelve-by-twelve-foot structure was destined to become Caren's creative refuge. Covered in vines and adorned with hanging baskets, the shed fits comfortably into the garden, an artful feature that comes close to being a "folly," Caren says. "It has been my space—as an art studio and as my nest—where I can work on projects."

Thanks to the property's terracing, the shed sits on a concrete foundation, similar to a daylight basement. Caren tidied that up ▶ 104

▲ Like butterflies alighting slender branches, the coral-pink blooms of a spring-flowering dogwood are confection for the eyes.

accentuate with ornamentation

Art objects can add new interest to a quiet corner of the landscape.

Well-placed ornamentation gives your garden a point of view. Its presence adds dimension and perspective, whether as a focal point to draw the eye through the landscape or as a subtle way to highlight or accentuate the plant palette. And as some gardeners are quick to joke, while plants may be fleeting, artwork has permanence.

The backyard environment may welcome a large-scale leaf cast in stone, a moss-covered figure tucked beneath the leaves of a giant hosta, or a trio of eight-foot columns salvaged from an old porch. When incorporating decorative accents into the garden, it's important to adhere to a unified palette. If you place containers throughout the beds or along the edge of a porch, select one finish, be it terra-cotta or a high-fire

▲ A scene from the golden garden reveals tufts of dazzling Japanese sweet flag (*Acorus gramineus*), a fitting "nest" for a sculpted hosta leaf by artists David Lewis and George Little.

glaze. Similarly, concentrate furniture together for impact of form, color, or material.

You can use ornaments to create a mood, be it restful and intimate or lively and energetic. Here are some ideas to guide you.

Juxtaposed Textures and Finishes:
Plants and artwork should compatibly coexist in the landscape, subtly complementing or dramatically contrasting to communicate the designer's intent. Use shiny, matte, or patterned ornaments to provide an eye-catching counterpoint to leaves, bark, and blossoms. Or, if you have a glittering gazing ball, make sure it's placed where it can reflect something equally dazzling, such as the ebony-colored blades of black mondo grass. A metal trellis or arbor that's been exposed to the elements will take on a sandpaper-like rust finish; so don't let that weathered texture disappear into a sea of green plants. Instead, draw attention to the piece by training a brilliant flowering vine along its twisted structure.

Something a bit wacky, like your second-grader's art class effort, is ideal for the

vegetable patch or herb garden, where it will put a smile on your face each time you're harvesting salad ingredients. Plant choices should show off the best of your ornamentation for an artful equation more delightful than its individual elements. Similarly, if your garden requires something useful, like stakes to hold tall lilies or dahlias, choose supports that are both decorative and utilitarian. "Having functional sculptural elements is one of my favorite things," Caren Anderson says. "When I don't need them, I stick them all in one spot as artwork."

Forms, Habits, and Proportions:
Ornamentation in the landscape offers numerous ways to meet gardening challenges. For example, art objects can add new interest to an unexciting corner of the landscape. Or if you have a spot where plants don't seem to thrive, consider it an opportunity to incorporate a large container display, place a birdbath, or tuck in a sculpture from a local artist. Use plants to offset sameness in a landscape. When a composition has too many plants with a mounded habit, add

spikes of interest with one or more tall ornaments. Alternately, you can use furniture or decorative accents to reinforce a design scheme. For example, when a border is filled with high-drama plants and bold foliage, you can use beefy furniture and oversized urns to reinforce the area's massive proportions.

Artistic Hierarchy: All artwork is not created equal. How much attention should a piece command? Choose an appropriate setting for each inanimate object in the landscape. A rustic watering can that you discovered at a Paris flea market belongs in a humble position, such as the back step or the doorway of a potting shed. Similarly, a sculpture should be elevated to its rightful place on a pedestal, surrounded by a supporting cast of plants and given accent lighting so you can enjoy it year round. Draw attention to a group of smaller items by displaying them as a unified collection, either on a shelf or ledge. Artifacts, antique or salvaged fragments, and small concrete figures are great fillers that will reside comfortably in a mixed border, delighting the viewer who catches a glimpse of them, but should not distract from the overall beauty of the planting.

▼ A contemplative figure of a seated woman with her arms drawn around her knees suggests a timeless serenity in the garden.

▲ Gnarled and weather-beaten, a hidden bench is discovered upon entering the golden garden.

▶ ▲ Looking like delicate jewels, the fronds of spring ferns unfurl in concert with the new green growth of a spruce tree.

▶ Lines from "Nothing Gold Can Stay," a Robert Frost poem, are carved into a stone commemorating a beloved child.

Hidden from view, the golden garden is a radiant secret place.

with vintage cupboards and shelves for pots and plants, extending one wall by adding a pop-out greenhouse. When daughter Amy and son David (named after his father) were young, they helped Mom tend to the vegetables, just beyond the structure. "When the kids got bigger, they didn't want to dig anymore and lost interest," she recalls. Only a small area for Caren's kitchen garden—herbs and salad greens— remains of the original vegetable patch.

Sunny and level, the spot once devoted to pumpkins, squash, and tomatoes seemed ideal for Caren's next project: a pond. She transformed the landscape by installing an irregular oval-shaped pool measuring about twenty-five by twenty feet. Edged with flagstone, which creates a nice pathway and seating area around its perimeter, the pond is large enough to hold a koi collection and numerous grasses and water-loving plants. "We made it tropical-looking, with cannas, bananas, melianthus (honey bush), and lots of grasses," Caren says. She relies on lavish, hardy tropicals adapted to Zones 7 and 8, such as the Japanese banana (*Musa basjoo*), giant-leafed gunnera (*Gunnera manicata*), and a variety of salmon-red and streaked cannas (*Canna* sp.), as well as dramatic perennials like New Zealand flax (*Phormium tenax*) and *Hosta* 'Sum and Substance'.

An architectural arbor supported by three concrete columns is a focal point beyond the water garden. Created by David Lewis and George Little, Bainbridge Island artists known for their concrete sculptures and inspired use of color, the arbor serves as a transparent screen at the edge of the garden. Paul's Himalayan musk, a pale pink rambling rose, climbs the periwinkle blue columns to the terra-cotta-colored arbor above. "The Little and Lewis arbor is like a frame to our view of Puget Sound and the Olympic Mountains," explains Caren.

Shades of periwinkle and blue provide a cool visual respite throughout the garden, showing up in subtle ways in both architecture (a pair of painted chairs) and horticulture (blue-tinged conifers and the elusive Himalayan blue poppy). Sometimes blue appears serendipitously, Caren adds. "I can have forget-me-nots, blue scilla, and blue corydalis all blooming at the same time, and I didn't even plan it."

Yet if Caren and David could single out one special color in their garden, it would be golden yellow. For them, the color symbolizes the enduring spirit of their daughter, Amy, who died of cancer in 1997. The spring after Amy's death, in tribute to this beloved young woman, Caren and David planted a golden garden, incorporating rare and common gold and yellow plants.

"I decided that it should be a golden garden," Caren recalls. "There's no real reason, other than that Amy loved sunflowers and was a sunny person. Amy made my life wonderful by her observations. She would say, 'You have no idea what kind of impact you have on people—by being a positive person who's enjoying life.'"

Hidden from view except for a small vine-covered arbor that serves as its entrance, the golden garden is a radiant secret place. A swing hangs between two trees, allowing visitors a place for rest and contemplation. "If you weren't told about the golden garden, you wouldn't know it was there, because you can't see it at all from the main garden," Caren says. "In spring when new foliage emerges, primroses bloom, and daffodils open up, it really does glow."

While it's sometimes difficult to put into words one's sentiments about a lost loved one, especially a child, some selected lines from a Robert Frost poem, "Nothing Gold Can Stay," speak volumes about the young woman memorialized by this garden. Island artist Molly Greist carved the lines into a large stone that sits in the golden garden—a gift to David and Caren from numerous friends. For anyone privileged to visit this garden and to be wrapped in the warm glow of soft yellow boughs and foliage, the chiseled poetry is a reminder of life's ephemeral, golden qualities. Truly Caren and David have created a cherished place. ✎

textured tapestry

an ornamental grass garden

an ornamental grass garden

◄ ◄ **Mirroring the movements of the sea, ample plantings of well-structured perennials and ornamental grasses meld with the saltwater channel beyond.**

▲ **The driveway stops midway down the property, where guests park and enter an Asian-inspired Arts-and-Crafts–style double gate.**

Before the breathtaking view from this garden comes into focus, brilliant swaths of perennials and lavish stands of ornamental grasses cast their alluring spell. For Alan Clasens and Jimene Smith, these fluid plantings expand the boundaries of their waterfront property, visually blending the elements of water and earth into one purely serene tableau.

In the early 1990s, the couple discovered the one-acre property while visiting friends in the area. They were attracted to the privacy offered by the sloping terrain, with a drive that wound through a wooded area to the house sited fifty feet below the road. The location's ever-changing views to the west overlook both the garden and a saltwater

channel sixty feet below, which separates Bainbridge Island from the Kitsap Peninsula. Here, the water may ripple gently one day and surge wildly the next.

Not surprisingly, the orientation of both home and property toward the sea served as a defining force in creating the dynamic garden tapestry that thrives here today. As the primary design inspiration, water has influenced everything from plant choices and placement to the outlines of planting beds and the course of the paths. With Al's help, avid gardener Jimene initially cultivated a traditional English cottage garden on the sloping waterside yard. After several years of tending to her landscape, Jimene realized that while her plants were thriving, the garden didn't feel unified. She considered consulting a professional designer. "I felt the garden needed some 'fine tuning' to create structure and cohesiveness," she explains.

Enter Jay Fossett, a garden designer with an intuitive approach who was recommended by a friend. Raised in the Baltimore area, where he helped his father install gardens designed by the famed landscape architect team of Wolfgang Oehme and James van Sweden, Jay borrows heavily from their influence. "I design to a setting larger than the garden itself," he explains. "I like to extend the lines of the garden beyond its edges."

Jay suggested the couple change the disordered look of ones and twos of various perennials and instead infuse their landscape with "masses and drifts of plants." The transformation required removing almost all of the existing herbaceous plant material from an 80-by-80-square-foot area between the house and the water before bringing in a textured tapestry of new plant choices.

"This advice was much more drastic than the 'fine tuning' I was looking for," says Jimene. "But after the initial shock, Jay's vision ▶ 114

◀ ◀ At summer's peak, the swaths of blue fescue (*Festuca glauca*), crimson-tipped firetail persicaria, *Sedum* 'Autumn Joy', black-eyed Susan, and Russian sage draw the eye upward.

◀ ▲ Sun-loving perennials, including *Persicaria microcephala* 'Red Dragon', orange-and-scarlet streaked cannas, and merlot-tinged barberry, fill the artfully planted container garden on the upper deck.

◀ The woodland entry garden is populated by ferns, brunneras, and Japanese maples. Taking center stage are the dazzling yellow-gold spires of *Ligularia stenocephala* 'The Rocket', illuminated in the dappled light.

▲ A lower deck echoes the perennial garden's sunny spirit, with black-eyed Susan-filled planter boxes (*Rudbeckia fulgida* 'Goldsturm').

changing motion

That which at first appears static comes alive with motion.

In garden design, the dynamic element of rhythm creates a visual flow through a landscape. As a beat is to music, as choreographed steps are to a dance, rhythm animates a garden. That which at first appears static comes alive with motion.

We experience a physical sensation when something rustles or sways in the garden. We pause to appreciate movements, subtle or dramatic—flowing water, rippling leaves, a billowing flag, or clanging chimes—because they signal life's evanescent qualities. Such movements resonate as the way a garden responds to the earth's vital elements.

By the very act of creating a garden, we embrace the external forces of nature, most of which are out of our control. In addition to rays of sunlight and rain showers, the kinetic presence of wind and breeze in our landscapes is important to channel—as movement—in a planting scheme.

It's rewarding to see how climatic changes affect the garden, something we can't help but notice, whether there are extreme gusts or light flurries flowing through our trees, shrubs, and perennials. When we intentionally design the garden to capture these movements, we infuse an otherwise commonplace landscape with vitality.

The choices of plants that can catch the airflow, gently dance, or furiously shake are endless. Perennials with tall, slender stems ripple like the fringe on a banner (think of a vibrant stand of daylilies or crocosmia).

Fluffy inflorescences of maiden grass undulate above the plant's finely textured blades—and the overall effect is a seductive rhythm. The leaves of a graceful beech tree shimmer like sequins on an evening gown. Seedpods on poppies rattle and whisper as autumn arrives. The natural symphony of motion and sound energizes any landscape.

Beyond individual plants, the visual suggestion of animation or motion can also be incorporated into the overall template of a garden. This metaphor of movement can be expressed in the repetition of organic forms, the course of a sinuous path, or the sensual outlines of beds and borders. Alternating shapes, the gradual widening or narrowing of a space, the regular spacing of trees—all can convey movement.

When the tiny gravel in a Zen garden is raked into concentric circles, movement appears. When "streams" of large, smooth, black stones fill a long gully or trench, the sense of running water is implied. The sequence of round stepping stones spaced through a cushioned ground of baby's tears invigorates the scene and helps direct the viewer's eye through the garden.

Movement in an abundant garden is essential. It's the organic rhythm, the fluid characteristic that every garden needs in order to come to life for those who enjoy it.

▶ The lively heads of *Lysimachia clethroides*, also called gooseneck loosestrife, display a sense of movement even when the wind is still.

▲ A glass bowl rests in a rusted steel frame where it captures rainwater. The modern birdbath is showcased against a coppery stand of feather reed grass (*Calamagrostis x acutiflora* 'Karl Foerster').

"A cultivated garden shouldn't compete with nature."

was contagious and we adopted his plan. What sold me was the multiseason interest of ornamental grasses and the particular perennials that Jay chose. With the brief blooming cycle of many of my English garden perennials, the hunt for fillers was endless."

The water, says Jay, was the garden's most obvious influence. "A cultivated garden shouldn't compete with nature. Instead, I wanted to play to that natural view and to have the garden be its introduction." Jay marked out a central pathway, one that softly twists as it moves away from the house, down the slope and through the garden.

He designed flowing beds for mass plantings, which emulate water-inspired swirls and crests. "We wanted to mimic the movement and energy of the view—and the waves," says Jay. "When you're in the garden, you feel as if you're walking on a grassy beach." The new scheme also retained a 500-square-foot oval lawn area that accommodates outdoor seating: a green-carpeted garden room wrapped on all sides by foliage, stems, and blades.

The design begins with a foundation of prominent winter-interest plants such as hybrid witch hazels (*Hamamelis* x *intermedia* 'Pallida' and 'Arnold Promise'). The lovely vase-shaped shrubs command attention, positioned at turns in the main path. Jay added evergreen plants such as *Nandina domestica* interspersed with *Euphorbia palustris* to fill in empty spaces near the home's foundation and along the edges of an exterior staircase. "I love the way these two plants weave together," Jays says, admiring the nandina's red berries and the euphorbia's yellow-green bracts.

Before planting the perennials, clients and designer installed thousands of spring-blooming bulbs, creating huge drifts of daffodils such as 'King Alfred', a pure yellow heirloom variety, and 'Salome', a creamy petaled flower with an apricot-salmon cup. Fragrant, multistemmed white 'Thalia' daffodils border the pathway. Species tulips, crocuses, and grape hyacinths add enchanting highlights of color and form. Early in the season, the garden is blanketed with shades of yellow, cream, peach, and violet. "Coming out of winter, the bulbs introduce spring with a splash—they're a sharp burst of color that wakens the senses," Jay points out.

Later, as the grasses and perennials begin to obscure the fading bulbs, the garden resembles irregular tracts of prairie land, as seen from a bird's-eye view. Clusters of ornamental grasses exhibit fountains, sprays, and plumes of textures fine, medium, and dense, all of which add a metallic glimmer to the landscape. Jay values grasses for their fluid forms and multiseason interest (he recommends cutting back the grasses in the early spring, which allows the garden to retain the attractive blades and seed heads throughout winter). "Grasses give more movement to a garden than any other perennial," he adds. "The interesting things, to me, are the lines they create."

Commanding attention are numerous choice grasses, including blue oat grass (*Helictotrichon sempervirens*), switch grass (*Panicum virgatum*), maiden grass (*Miscanthus sinensis* 'Gracillimus'), fountain grass (*Pennisetum alopecuroides*), and feather reed grass (*Calamagrostis* x *acutiflora* 'Karl Foerster'). "A little breeze and the whole mass of grasses moves," Jay points out.

Grasses relate companionably with drifts of perennials and ornamental shrubs, creating color-infused masses that emerge in

"Grasses give more movement to a garden than any other perennial."

▼ Hidden amid feather reed grasses and a low-planted mass of blue fescue, a weathered cedar bench gives Al and Jimene the feeling they are visiting a windswept coastal beach.

Varying the heights of plants creates the illusion of movement.

▲ The spherical rusted ironwork cage offers an unpretentious touch of ornamentation.

► From a shaded spot next to the house, the garden flows toward the intense western sunlight, visually igniting the golden petals of a massed planting of black-eyed Susans.

a continual wave of new blooms. Jay contrasts lazy growth habits with upright ones, varying the heights of adjacent plants to create the illusion of movement. *Sedum* 'Autumn Joy', *Geranium macrorrhizum*, firetail persicaria (*Persicaria amplexicaulis* 'Firetail'), purple coneflower (*Echinacea purpurea*), gooseneck loosestrife (*Lysimachia clethroides*) , joe-pye weed (*Eupatorium purpureum*), bluebeard (*Caryopteris* x *clandonensis*), Russian sage (*Perovskia atriplicifolia*), purple salvia

▼ Like delicate tumbleweeds, the spent globelike blooms of ornamental alliums add graphic impact to the garden, long after their purple hue fades.

▲ Resembling the tufts on a chenille robe, this pink-tinged bed of *Sedum* 'Autumn Joy' has an irresistible, tactile quality.

▶ Its black-brown buttonlike center punctuates the yellow rays of this enduring summer perennial, *Rudbeckia fulgida* 'Goldsturm'.

▶ Far right, from top: The dried ball-shaped bloom of an ornamental allium; purple coneflower; a fantastical garden "bird" made from a recycled spade; and a pink Japanese anemone.

(*Salvia verticillata* 'Purple Rain'), fall asters (*Aster* x *frikartii*), black-eyed Susan (*Rudbeckia fulgida* 'Goldsturm'), 'Stella de Oro' daylilies, and *Yucca filamentosa* 'Adam's Needle' are each given their own defined place in the overall framework of this garden.

"I like to change the heights of each plant section and alternate textures," Jay explains. "You can see the whole garden because the dynamic of different plant heights allows you to see into the planting beds."

By late summer, the soft path to the beach is nearly hidden by the tallest stalks and stems, making a journey through the garden a ▶ 122

animate
the garden

Select plants that
bring height, energy,
and motion.

Designer Jay Fossett has a passion for large planting areas that imbue the landscape with a compelling quality defined not by individual plants, but by bold impressions of color, texture, and form. He doesn't rely on tiny details; rather, on unforgettable pairings of succulent shapes, fine filaments, and rhythmic planting patterns.

To animate the abundant garden, you can borrow from a similar design vocabulary, one that uses emphasis and balance as its tools. With "emphasis," some plants come to the foreground, while others take a supporting role. For "balance," make sure that strong elements in one area of the garden are offset by equally dramatic ones elsewhere.

Jay likens this approach to conducting an orchestra as it plays a classical score. "In a symphony, there is an interesting combination of fascinating people who have a mixture of dynamic talents. The orchestra has to have all these instruments, each playing a different role, in order to be successful."

The garden, he says, should embody this symphonic style. His design challenge:

"How many different elements can you use and yet have them all work in harmony?"

Here are some ideas for incorporating the magic of movement and animation in your garden.

Develop a Repertoire of Plants:
Base your plant selection on the scale of your house and the natural setting around it. Once you've selected the primary plants—those that provide structure and have multiseason interest—you can choose a second wave of plants to "star" in specific seasons. In Alan Clasens and Jimene Smith's garden, for example, masses of daffodils and narcissus command attention with their springtime floral displays.

Create a Basic Framework for Design:
Choose a template and follow it consistently throughout the garden. One method is to mirror the dominant lines of the house, extending the structure's outline or drawing key architectural shapes into the landscape

as a guide for shaping pathways, and planting beds and lawns. For example, the curve of a bay window might be echoed in the shape of a border. Alternately, you can borrow a framework for design from nature, which is how Jay was inspired to echo shapes from sea and sky in Al and Jimene's landscape.

Consider the Vertical Dimension:
Select plants that bring height, energy, and motion into the garden, and vary their

▲ Waves of color flow from one dramatic stand to the next, culminating at the shoreline beyond. The ornamental alliums that "float" above the other perennials infuse this planting scheme with rhythmic bursts of energy.

placement for impact. Even if surrounded by tall buildings on every side, your garden will respond to daily and seasonal climate changes. Watch how breezes move through the garden, and capture that energy by placing fluid plants where currents flow. Notice where the sun rises and sets in relation to your landscape, and choose trees, shrubs, grasses, and other perennials that will reflect the morning light or absorb sunset's glow. Red and purple foliage turns flame-like when backlit. As the sun's rays shine through fringed tassels of maiden grass, the garden will shimmer.

▼ Calm white and intense blue join for a duet of gentle movement. The border of creamy white *Lysimachia clethroides* relates well with a stand of blue-flowering *Caryopteris* x *clandonensis.*

The beauty of this garden is that everything is so well orchestrated.

▲ Raspberry-red spikes of aptly named firetail persicaria (*Persicaria amplexicaulis* 'Firetail') erupt in this singular performance of color and form.

▶ The ball-shaped seed heads of *Allium* 'Globemaster' are showcased against some of the garden's signature plants, including feather reed grass (*Calamagrostis* x *acutiflora* 'Karl Foerster'), velvety-purple Russian sage (*Perovskia atriplicifolia*), and yet-to-bloom *Sedum* 'Autumn Joy'.

breathtaking experience. The setting sun illuminates the bronzy tones of seed heads, adding its glow to the landscape. Dozens of ball-shaped ornamental alliums, which have gone to seed but remain as graphic accents, punctuate the scene. "I love the stark contrast between the tall stems and the circles formed by the alliums," Jay observes. "It shows off the true architecture of the plants."

Avid participants in the design and installation of their garden, Al and Jimene continue to experiment with plants as the landscape matures and changes. "The best, yet most difficult, aspect of a garden like this is that you must avoid impulse buying," says Jimene. "A new plant candidate must pass rigorous scrutiny before you commit to planting a mass of them. The beauty of this garden is that everything is so well orchestrated; plants grow simultaneously and age gracefully. While these mass plantings are dynamic, they also create serenity. Your eye doesn't jump from plant to plant. It's a soothing garden." ∿

dreaming big

an exotic tropical garden

an exotic tropical garden

L inda Cochran tends to her outlandish garden paradise with a studied focus, selecting trees, shrubs, and perennials for their bold architecture and dynamic foliage. "My primary design principle is to follow the form of a plant's leaves," she explains. "For me, form comes before color."

Hers is a high-contrast design style. Linda prefers the dramatic over the understated—a philosophy evident in the enormous foliage, contrasting textures, and intense jewel tones that surround her home located on Bainbridge Island's sunny, southern tip.

This self-taught gardener experiments with any plant that exhibits a hardy disposition for her Zone 8 garden and its typical cycle of wet,

◄◄ The grand entry gate opens onto a larger-than-life-sized landscape with tropical and exotic plants, including a stand of hardy banana (*Musa basjoo*) and the blue-tinged honey bush (*Melianthus major*), admired for its oversized, serrated foliage.

◄ Dwarfed by her botanical acquisitions, Linda is a hands-on gardener who ardently pursues new specimens from far-flung locations.

◄◄ These chairs offer both seating and a colorful lime zest to the sunny patio. A painted terra-cotta egg provides perfect plum-purple color.

▲ A container-sized water garden offers a cool counterpoint to a selection of hot-spectrum blooms, including *Crocosmia* 'Jenny' and *Crocosmia* x *crocosmiiflora* 'Emily McKenzie'.

temperate winters and warm, dry summers. She defies zonal limitations in search of exotic specimens from around the globe, showcasing them in a stunning garden that attracts visitors from equally distant places. Lush masses of tropical plants and hardy selections that look tropical wrap around the Southwest-style home where Linda lives with her husband, David Jurca, and fifteen-year-old daughter, Jennifer.

Linda has spent the past decade creating her landscape, drawing from her fascination with unusual plants to nurture an otherworldly landscape, one that resembles an arboretum thriving in some faraway, tropical locale. Cannas, bamboo, hardy bananas, palms, gunnera, euphorbia, and crocosmia grow here in audacious masses.

Called "Froggy Bottom," Linda's garden is not the classic Northwest landscape of evergreen ferns, conifers, and broad-leafed shrubs ▶ **133**

▲ The electric blue urn creates a dynamic focal point among some favorite palms, including *Trachycarpus fortunei*, the hardy windmill palm. In the background, the shade-giving arbor supports a lavish display of kiwi vines (*Actinidia deliciosa*), while in the foreground, variegated Jacob's ladder (*Polemonium caeruleum* 'Brise d'Anjou') softly obscures the urn's base.

"My primary design principle is to follow the form of a plant's leaves. For me, form comes before color."

speaking of patterns

Be they playful, sensuous, or meditative, patterns give a garden its personality.

Abundant garden design relies on enduring visual cues to create a pleasing context, a point of reference for the landscape. These can be organic symbols—in the form of ornamental plants—or inorganic ones, such as sculpture or architecture. When thoughtfully placed in the residential landscape, these elements lend definition and order, creating a design pattern, a vocabulary of forms, colors and materials—each of which reflect the individual style of both garden and garden maker.

Be they playful, sensuous, or meditative, patterns give a garden its personality and character and provide the framework that makes it possible to "read" a garden. Graphic or amorphous, such components are a visual "Morse code" of sorts that can communicate the garden's mood.

Forms: Pleasing forms—derived from a favorite tree, the shape of decorative latticework, or square urns for the container garden—register and resonate with us visually. When forms reappear throughout the garden, they create a pattern that conveys unity and rhythm, hallmarks of design.

You can use an archetypal shape or form, such as a diamond or ovoid form, as the landscape's design motif. Or choose a key plant habit such as weeping, arching, tufted, or mounded. When such a visual cue is established—and then repeated, it creates a pattern that leads the eye through each space, whether the motif helps define the arc of a mixed border, the square grid on a fence, or the zigzag of a path.

Such patterns provide cohesion for the larger garden and amplify the importance of smaller spaces as accents and relief. As patterns emerge throughout the landscape, they can be enlarged, rotated, multiplied, or inverted. A bay window may determine the shape of a curved trellis. The planting of columnar shrubs may mirror the architectural columns on a front porch. A circular patio can give way to an equally round patch of lawn.

Colors: Colors further emphasize the power of a pattern, as a single shade of paint splashed on doors, gates, walls, or furniture. Or, perhaps your preferred foliage color is blue-gray, so you highlight the landscape

with blue-gray plants clustered at significant spots, so as to indicate a change in levels or a transition from public into private spaces.

Materials: Patterns are best conveyed through the simplest of materials—such as using square or rectangular concrete pavers to cover the garden floor with an arrangement that borrows from the home's interior mood—and further blends the line between the interior and exterior environment. By choosing and repeating a single type of pottery finish, such as Italian terra-cotta or a Malaysian blue-green glaze, the garden's overall design is reinforced.

▲ In this mixed border, favorite perennials with similar, arching sprays of long stems and slender foliage are repeated.

▶ These stone steps lead the eye toward a soft circle, planted with silver spear grass (*Achnatherum calamagrostis*) and a sculpture of a lioness and her cubs.

▲ From top: A fantastical dragon at the edge of a pot; a pink-tinged foxtail lily (*Eremurus* sp.); an imposing lioness, hiding amid the grasses.

such as rhododendrons. Perhaps this garden is so successful because Linda borrows views—and the towering proportions—from the mature deciduous trees that surround her island property, including big-leaf maples, willows, cottonwoods and alders.

Within the perimeter of her one-and-a-half-acre garden, Linda exploits the best features of her nonnative herbaceous and woody plants. For example, instead of allowing the common Empress tree (*Paulownia tomentosa*) to produce lilac flowered clusters, Linda cuts the tree to the ground each spring, sacrificing the blooms so it produces foliage the size of dinner plates. Likewise, she coppices the golden catalpa tree (*Catalpa bignonioides* 'Aurea'), in order to stimulate larger and lusher leaves.

When visitors see the thriving, but unfamiliar specimens in her garden, they want to emulate its look and feel. Fans covet such rarities as the

◄ Within a dynamic display of foliage plants, a sculpted sphere is wrapped with a terra-cotta serpent. The metallic, venous foliage of *Brunnera macrophylla* 'Jack Frost' glows in contrast to the dark clay.

▲ Against the peacock blue-streaked wall, Linda displays a profusion of plants with interesting leaf shapes or purplish blooms. Providing a fresh canopy of lime green above is the golden catalpa tree (*Catalpa bignonioides* 'Aurea').

▲ A majestic heron stands sentry at
Linda and David's garden entrance.
The copper detailing of bird and foliage
has taken on a verdigris patina.

▶ Bamboo and bananas are hardy in
this Zone 8 garden. Layered in front of
them are plants with strong geometric
shapes, including honey bush (*Melianthus
major*) and rice-paper plant (*Tetrapanax
papyrifer*). Containers display a variegated
agave (*Agave americana* 'Marginata')
and *Cussonia paniculata*, whose leaves
resemble oversized puzzle pieces.

"My whole vision
was to have a secret
garden, as seen
through a gate."

big-leaf magnolia (*Magnolia macrophylla*), which has large, oval leaves
and reaches heights of fifty feet, the Himalayan giant lily (*Cardiocrinum
giganteum*), an unusual bulb with eighteen-inch-long leaves, or
Darmera peltata, an herbaceous perennial with umbrella-like leaves.

Plants partner with architectural elements for strongest effect.
Fuchsia-colored Adirondack chairs, acid-green armchairs, a teal trellis,
three-foot-tall painted eggs, and concrete walls glazed in shades of
peacock and terra-cotta offer a vibrant palette that holds its own
against strong foliage forms and surreal plant proportions.

Linda's story inspires anyone who fantasizes about jumping off the
fast-track treadmill and into a plant-centered lifestyle. A former corporate
attorney, she retired from a Seattle legal practice about fifteen years
ago, turning to gardening as her vocation. While raising her daughter,
Linda has expanded her horticultural vocabulary and design acumen
with the ardor of a trial attorney.

When Linda and David bought their house in 1993, they were
attracted to its private location and spacious architecture; the
surrounding property had been untouched. The residence had been
built by a contractor from Arizona, a surprisingly appropriate fit for
the garden that followed, as Linda began to seek out exotic plants,
including desert-like selections for her drought-tolerant entry garden.

"It was horrible. All that was here was a drainage ditch with a
culvert over it," Linda recounts. She worked with Bainbridge Island-
based landscape architect Bart Berg to begin refining the outside
areas close to her home, planning patios, walls, a courtyard, and gated
entrance. "My whole vision was to have a secret garden, as seen
through a gate," she explains. Designed by Berg and Diane Harris,
an artist, and custom-fabricated by metalsmith Ernie Blevins, a
wrought-iron and copper gate serves as the garden's main portal.
Exotic tetrapanax leaves and a giant heron embellish twin panels that
swing open, inviting visitors to walk beneath a Japanese roof and
into a garden that explodes with highly contrasted plant forms,
offset by a lush strolling lawn.

Linda was born in Iraq, where she lived until she was seven.
Her family then spent two years in Beirut, Lebanon. "I like warm
climates," she enthuses, which is reflected in her design decisions.
"Maybe that's why I like palms so much, too."

Middle Eastern memories inspired her selection of plants that
grow close to the equator, including several varieties of bamboo,
giant eucalyptus, and countless hardy palms. Pleated, fanned, spiked,
and feather-shaped, the leaves of Linda's palms lend a bold ▶ **138**

devise a pattern for your garden

Integrate a well-defined motif—or pattern—to unify a landscape.

If you have a landscape that lacks cohesion or seems like a series of unrelated parts, integrate a well-defined motif—or pattern—to unify its appearance. This exercise works well with both young and established landscapes.

Begin by performing what some designers call the "squint test," and observe your garden from a distance, squinting your eyes so that you see the landscape as *shapes* and *masses,* rather than individual plants. How do things read this way? Are they well-integrated or do they seem out of balance?

If that doesn't work for you, photograph your garden in black-and-white, a trick that removes the color from a scene and instead brings forms, outlines, and dark-light contrasts to the forefront.

Take note of the strongest components of your landscape and then seek ways to

▶ A medley of potted specimens gives Linda's terrace garden an ever-changing appearance. These desert and exotic plants present a pattern of succulent, stiff, swordlike and spiked shapes.

repeat and reinforce them. For example, a half-circle patio leading from the back porch may call for extending the form—as in the ripples from a pebble dropped into water—into a second curved shape around its perimeter, planted with shrubs and perennials. Or, look at the peak on your home's roofline and repeat it in an arbor or trellis to help move the eye from home into garden.

Linear and Bold: Linda Cochran pays close attention to both graphic foliage and a plant's overall form. She has developed her own "pattern"—a proven method of pairing plants. "I like to combine something linear with something big or broad," she explains. This approach accentuates leaf shapes over fleeting blooms, surrounding bold forms with finer textures to ensure that every plant receives the notice it deserves. As a result, the garden has a multidimensional quality and a dynamic energy.

For Linda, "linear" plants include evergreen bamboos, torch lilies (*Kniphofia* hybrids), sedges, and grasses, such as fifteen-foot-tall pampas grass (*Cortaderia*

selloana) and giant silver grass (*Miscanthus* 'Giganteus'), which reaches heights of ten to fourteen feet. Broad-leafed selections include hardy and tropical bananas, hybrid cannas, and Linda's golden catalpa tree.

Weeping Forms: Adding drama of their own are weeping trees that lend a fluid counterpoint to more upright plants. "I just like weeping trees—if I could have more of them, I would," Linda notes. A Camperdown elm (*Ulmus glabra* 'Camperdownii') is trained into an umbrella form, the branches of which reach to the ground and cast patterned shadows during the winter months. The landscape also features other weeping forms of favorite trees, including Japanese maples, a willow-leafed pear, a birch, and a large copper beech.

Color Patterns: Linda also favors high-contrast colors for pattern motifs, selecting intense tones to emphasize and accentuate her landscape. Because her plant choices are so strong on foliage, Linda uses vermillion, hot pink, acid green, teal, and peacock blue to play off the varying shades of green

leaves. When she wants to call attention to an area of the garden, Linda often relies on a can of brightly colored paint to accomplish the task. She's brought vibrant color to all sorts of surfaces, including terra-cotta egg sculptures, garden furniture, and wooden gates and arbors.

Light and Shadow: There's an ever-changing element to Linda's garden, perpetuated by the sun's movement across the sky. As the light progresses from dawn to dusk, shadows add yet another type of pattern to the environment. The sunlight catches the alluring silhouettes of serrated and notched leaf forms, fine grasses, and tropical blooms, throwing moody shadows against the terra-cotta and bright blue-stained walls.

▲ Landscape architect Bart Berg worked with Linda and David to design and install a raised cistern-like pool and petal-shaped fountain, a calming focal point. Framing the scene are honey bush (*Melianthus major*), fountain grass (*Pennisetum orientale* 'Tall Tails'), *Verbena bonariensis*, dark-leafed dahlias, and a mass of red hybrid cannas.

▲ Crafted from bamboo poles lashed together with twine, a gate and arbor at the far edge of the garden offer a Southeast Asian touch. A shocking-pink stand of gladiolas in front of it adds pizzaz.

Linda resists formality by interpreting traditional design styles with her own twist.

geometric form to the mixed borders. Among others, she grows the windmill palm (*Trachycarpus fortunei*), Mediterranean fan palm (*Chamaerops humilis*), Chilean wine palm (*Jubaea chilensis*), and the South American pindo palm (*Butia capitata*).

Complementing these striking horticultural specimens is a soothing cistern, installed along the west side of Linda and David's home. Designed by Bart Berg, the pool measures approximately ten by four feet and is elevated eighteen inches above the ground so that its ledge provides additional seating along a paved patio. Emerging from the water is a blue-tinged bloom, sculpted by David Lewis and George Little. Water drips from the flower into the rectangular pool below, adding a sultry melody to the mood-setting landscape.

Considerably wider than it is deep, the garden spans a full 10,000 feet. To accentuate the garden's rectangular dimensions, Linda relies on axial lines, ensuring that anyone standing at one end will see through to an interesting plant, sculpture, or architectural element at a terminal point in the distance. These sight lines are also revealed at secondary points perpendicular to the main garden, allowing the eye to move through shallow and deeper spaces, and providing vistas to enjoy from afar. Even though they may be partially obscured by fronds and foliage, the permanent elements—gates, artifacts, art objects, and walls—also conform to these axial lines.

When it comes to color, Linda skips most anything with white blooms, instead choosing heat-seeking tones of gold and chartreuse. "I want the garden to feel warm," she says. "I have a few variegated plants, but I use yellow variegation rather than white."

Linda brightens the landscape with golden plants. When repeated throughout the garden, these sunny elements are a useful design tool that adds a visual order to the landscape's high-energy personality. The golden form of black locust tree (*Robinia pseudoacacia* 'Frisia') is one of her favorites. A trio of lemon-lime colored Monterey cypresses (*Cupressus macrocarpa*) unifies the landscape, adding splashes of gold against dark green foliage.

Informal crescents and curving bands of lawn provide another form of green, one that is a constant, fine-textured sea of calm amidst the copious foliage borders. "If I didn't have the lawn, I think it would feel too crowded here," Linda points out. "It maintains some openness in the garden."

In the side lawn, to the south of her home, Linda has carved out a circle garden which shelters a bronze sculpture of a lioness and her cubs, by artist Georgia Gerber. Appropriately surrounded by a showy

stand of silver spear grass (*Achnatherum calamagrostis*), the scene is reminiscent of the African plains. Drawing further attention to this focal point in the landscape are four columnar yews, planted in an irregular pattern around the vignette.

Linda resists formality by interpreting traditional design styles with her own twist. Where another gardener might clip a shrub into a symmetrical topiary, surrounding it with a tidy row of boxwood, Linda takes a slightly irreverent approach. She plants a stand of Ethiopian red bananas (*Ensete ventricosum*) and showcases it against a mass of yellow-streaked palm sedges (*Carex muskingumensis* 'Oehme'). The result is dazzling.

"I want my plants to have the room to develop their full potential," she explains. Having adopted flora from nearly every culture and continent, Linda lives large in her inspiring landscape. ✎

▲ In one of several container ponds, a film of duckweed (*Lemna minor*) creates a lime-green surface pattern. The jewel-like glass balls and delicate 'Stargazer' lilies become a spontaneous still-life.

"I want my plants to have the room to develop their full potential."

cottage bouquet

a nostalgic rose garden

a nostalgic rose garden

◄◄ **A brick pathway, punctuated by roses, leads to the home's back garden, curving alongside the concrete-and-brick wall.**

▲ **A timeworn patina was given to the concrete wall by adding a brick cap and inserting sections of cut brick to suggest age.**

Exuberant borders, playful artwork, and comfortable furnishings infused with vibrant colors define and energize Liz and Peter Robinson's cottage garden. In this landscape, blooms are queen and fragrance is king. "It's just bliss," Liz says of time spent among her cherished roses, of which she grows 150. "I don't care if I remember the name of a flower, but I do remember its scent and the first time I ever saw it."

While she adores English boxwood for the architectural form it contributes to her garden spaces, Liz relies on her rose collection to give her garden its sense of abundance. Roses old and new climb arbors, cover trellises, and clamber along the side of a weathered shed,

"I don't care if I remember the name of a flower, but I do remember its scent and the first time I ever saw it."

◀◀ This rustic shed is the ideal "wall" against which to grow perennials, herbs, and both climbing and rambling roses, including 'Flutterbye', a pink-and-yellow single rose, and 'Evangeline', a creamy white-and-pink rose.

◀ Liz Robinson is drawn to her garden where she combines exuberant cottage flowers in vibrant shades. She enjoys a rare moment of rest, seated next to a rusted metal arbor created by her son-in-law, Steve Smyth.

▲ Leaning against a geranium-red gate, Peter Robinson shares his wife's passion for restoring older properties and giving their children and grandchildren a welcoming place to call home.

offering a profusion of blooms in a tapestry of colors. Combined with tall perennials and undemanding herbs, the informal plantings soften the edges of paths, walls, and fences of this carefree garden.

Married forty-nine years, Liz and Peter have owned and tended many gardens in the Seattle area. During the past thirty years they have lived on Bainbridge Island. While each of her residences has been difficult to leave, Liz says the promise of creating a new garden always inspires her with dreams of growing more beloved plants. "I just like to dig," she confides. "Gardening gives me a reason to go outside."

Eight years ago the Robinsons bought and renovated a circa 1900 army warehouse where mules were once shod, turning it into an inviting cottage with high ceilings and plenty of light-lending windows. Painted cheery yellow with geranium-red doors, the well-loved structure is indeed the central element of Liz's garden, a fitting backdrop to nostalgic flowers like roses, peonies, poppies, foxglove, delphiniums, and swaths of lavender.

In about one-third of an acre, Liz has created a delightful escape for friends and family who visit, including her five beloved grandchildren, who frequently spend time in the garden with "Nana." "Children and gardening put life into perspective," she observes, recalling the therapeutic value of gardening when she had five youngsters under twelve at ▶ 149

▲ The blooms from Liz and Peter's garden inspire lovely bouquets. Specimens, from top: the single-blooming 'Flutterbye' rose; a cupped peony with double-pink blooms and fringed golden center; pure white bearded irises; and 'Robusta', a thorny raspberry red rugosa.

paint the garden

The quality of light may offer one of the best clues for selecting the garden's leaf and floral palette.

When you define the garden's color palette—highlighting plants, architecture, and artwork with a scheme that's intentionally controlled or diverse—you give an abundant garden an unforgettable personality. All gardens begin with a spectrum of green shades, the chlorophyll-enriched building blocks of our trees, shrubs, vines, ground covers, and perennials. Beyond that, thanks to the horticulture world's endless supply of new plant introductions, we can draw from an increasingly varied offering of foliage hues. Burgundy, chocolate, blue-green, silver, gold, and variegated leaves play an important role in coloring a garden.

Beyond foliage, we rely on the floral divas of each season, and here's where color often makes its strongest statement. Some gardens can carry the exuberance of a rainbow effect, a scheme that fine artists describe as polychromatic. By design, other landscapes are limited to a singular palette, such as the famous white garden designed by Vita Sackville-West at Sissinghurst.

Between these two extremes are well-planned landscapes with their color schemes realized by three to five hues, contrasting or blending tones for greater appeal.

Your home's interior colors or the wardrobe you typically wear may inspire your choice of garden palette. Favorite paint colors or textile prints can find their way into the garden maker's psyche, subconsciously influencing one's decision to reach for the magenta-flowered Cape fuchsia (*Phygelius* x *rectus*), rather than the pale lemon-flowered form. A home's architecture provides another point of reference: a Tuscan-inspired residence calls for sunset shades of gold, apricot, and melon. A humble farmhouse suggests a free-spirited collection of old-fashioned pastels. The cooler shades of lime, blue, and purple may reflect a contemporary or modernistic style.

The quality of light in your area may offer one of the best clues for selecting the garden's leaf and floral palette. In coastal areas, where the air is moist and frequently heavy with mist, the light is filtered, making softer shades recede and vibrant shades appear cooler. Where the open sky feels endless, such as in the high desert and plains regions, there's a saturated quality to colors, one that intensifies with extended periods of bright sunlight or rain, giving favorite hues a depth and richness.

Use massed plantings of a favorite perennial to echo colors that appear elsewhere in the landscape (both in your own garden and from borrowed views), giving them more momentum. You can keep the color palette more intense in certain spots, allowing dominant shades to define a focal point or view. Muted tones help the eye transition between the bolder elements, providing a restful visual pause.

Once you've given certain colors a starring role in the landscape, use them to guide your decisions for nonplant material. Edit and enhance the palette with painted structures, furniture, and artifacts. Containers, gates, and seat cushion and umbrella fabrics are elements just as important to your garden's color story as are blooms.

▲ Annual nasturtiums fill a concrete planter box, reflecting the garden's signature yellow-and-red color scheme.

▶ An informal balance between plants and ornamentation is struck here: a pale pink foxglove stands next to a concrete-sculpted version of the flower. The garnet-hued gate picks up on the color value of nearby reddish bricks.

home. "What's important is the nourishing and love that you give to the plants and children—you get back what you put into them."

To establish her cottage garden, Liz ripped out overgrown blackberries, improved the soil, and brought cherished plants from her prior home, including more than a dozen boxwoods and rose shrubs she'd been given by oldest daughter, Barbara Smyth. Liz and Peter replaced a crumbling blacktop drive with a brick pathway that curves alongside and around the house. Peter also constructed an openwork lattice fence to span the back border of the garden. "It's beautiful and

◄ A utilitarian bucket serves as an impromptu vase for quickly gathered blooms, cut from perennials and rose shrubs that grow against the latticework fence.

▲ *Bonjour*, declares the welcoming turquoise sap bucket where Liz displays cut flowers, such as 'Amber Queen', a golden floribunda rose, and 'Gertrude Jekyll', a fragrant double-pink English rose.

▲ Charming botanical scenes occur in unexpected places, such as on a weathered bench in the garden. Here, Liz fills wine bottles, a cracked terra-cotta pot, and small glass jars with cut rose blooms.

▶ The rustic clothesline, pins, and a galvanized wash bucket complement a glorious display of roses.

it keeps the deer away from my roses," Liz points out. Allowed to weather to a soft silver-gray, the fence blends comfortably with foliage and flowers alike.

The garden is further enclosed with two very different "walls" on either side. To the west, Liz and Peter have appropriated the side of an adjacent shed, once used to store coal. Climbing roses like 'Evangeline' and 'Flutterbye' grow against the weathered wood, which reflects ▶ 154

tools for garden design

The magic of color is at the gardener's fingertips.

Survey your landscape and identify areas that need resuscitation. Perhaps there's a spot that's lost its luster, where the plants seem a little lifeless. One excellent way to infuse an abundant feeling into a challenging place in the garden is to tackle the color palette.

Color can energize a collection of common plants, as Liz Robinson has done by painting a pair of Adirondack chairs in the same shade of rosy crimson that appears in a nearby self-sown stand of red valerian (*Centranthus ruber*). Color conveys choice and tells a story: garden makers have the entire color wheel at their fingertips. Select a specific palette. Lure the eye. Brighten a dark spot. Create a mysterious effect with moody hues. Explore the magic of color.

Here are some color ideas, inspired by many of the landscapes featured in *The Abundant Garden*.

Create a Harmonious Color Scheme:

Select two or more favorite colors that work well together in flowers, foliage, or structures. Liz Robinson relies on equally intense shades of red and yellow, high-energy hues that make her smaller garden appear larger and create a cohesive interplay between her home and garden. Other landscapes may benefit from subtler choices, relying on quiet colors to create a restful, nurturing feeling. Periwinkle blue and violet are examples, seen readily in the tonal blooms of *Hydrangea macrophylla*.

Use Common Foliage Shades to Unify Nongreen Landscape Elements:

Predominantly green plants help transition and blend sections of the garden and give them interest, even when there's nothing in bloom. When incorporating variegated foliage into the garden, avoid clashing plants with white-and-green leaves and those with cream-and-green leaves.

Provide a Backdrop for Plants:

This design strategy works for both dark and light plants. For instance, a golden conifer will glow when placed in front of a dark evergreen hedge. Unless it's surrounded by lighter toned plants, such as silvery blue wheatgrass (*Elymus magellanicus*), a plum-colored black elder (*Sambucus nigra*) "reads" as a dark blob.

Play with the Basic Rules of a Color Wheel:

You can devise a monochromatic scheme (in gardening terms, this might translate into a garden with blooms, berries, and bark in coral and salmon colors). Or, use a complementary statement in which colors opposite each other on the color wheel punch up a dull spot. Enjoy experimenting. While red and green are opposites on the color wheel, their horticultural equivalent is more interesting when plants of analogous colors (those next to each other on the color wheel) are placed together: plants with lime-colored foliage paired with burgundy-colored ones. Plants of analogous colors offer a pleasing visual harmony when all cool tones (purple, blue, and violet) or warm tones (red, orange, and yellow) are grown together.

▲ When Liz floats attractive blooms in her glazed birdbath, she may be inspired to group the same plants together in the garden, such as the pink rose, sapphire-blue geranium, and lime-colored lady's mantle intermingled here.

▶ Blue delphiniums inject a finishing detail to the pink-and-red hues of Liz's rose borders.

the neighborhood's historic feeling. Liz fears the structure will be torn down one day, but in the meantime, she happily treats it as a garden wall.

Along the east side of her garden, Liz designed a six-foot concrete wall, scheming with her contractor about ways to make it resemble something from an aging English garden. They added a brick cap and faced the concrete with small sections of cut brick to suggest an old edifice—for much less than the cost of a solid brick enclosure. Over time, the concrete wall has developed a patina, giving it a sense of history. It's an undemanding backdrop for ornamental shrubs, roses, and the perennial border, not to mention a favored spot for the family cat to sun himself.

Like many passionate gardeners, Liz admits to having a weakness for plants. She generously urges Peter to take in a game of golf so she can sneak another rose shrub from her car into the soil, undetected. "I buy plants because I just can't resist them—and then I make room for them," Liz proclaims. "I plant as I go because I'm greedy!"

While she claims to have no master plan, it's clear that Liz's effortless design style reflects an artistic sensibility. She attributes her love of color to a childhood in pre-World War II China (her father worked there for an international oil company). "I love Oriental rugs, which is why I love putting colors together," Liz says. "Plus, my mother lived part of her childhood in India and her father was a dealer in Persian rugs." A lifetime surrounded with intense patterns and hues is translated into Liz's own vibrant garden palette.

Using blooms rather than strands of wool, Liz recreates the dynamic shades of tapestries and carpets from her upbringing in the Far East. She pairs scarlet rose blooms with cobalt delphiniums and deep purple salvias, sprinkling the combination with accents of pure yellow. "I like to use intense colors—the eyes see these first," she explains. "Then I add less intense colors around them." Her confident choices begin with the primary tones, in particular the yellow paint colors that she and Peter chose for the house and a backyard shed. Trained on standards, a golden pair of 'Amber Queen' floribunda roses bloom all summer long. "They're never the same from one year to the next," she says. "But I'm always so happy to see when they first start blooming."

Against the buildings, Liz's flowering shrubs, roses, and perennials look more vibrant, with many of the rich crimson blooms echoing the red doors and garden chairs. A raspberry-red rugosa rose, called 'Robusta', explodes with intensity in one spot. Red poppies follow dark red peonies as the season moves from spring to summer.

Intense patterns and hues are translated into Liz's vibrant garden palette.

▲ The rosy red paint that coats the doors to Liz and Peter's house is repeated in this casual wooden garden chair; a punch of purple in the form of a hardy geranium tumbling over the stone wall provides high contrast.

Liz gardens with an intuitive style learned from a lifetime of puttering in the soil. The hands-on lessons learned are important ones, proving to her that rules are made to be broken. For example, Liz loves growing tall perennials in the front of a garden border rather than relegating them to the back row. "Especially if they smell good," she observes. She prefers ornamentation to be placed spontaneously rather than formally, hanging a pierced tin sap bucket that reads BONJOUR on an existing nail and filling it with cut roses. "I'm not a reader of garden books because I don't want to find out that I've done anything wrong," she confides.

Liz seems as enchanted with her precious landscape as those who visit it on local garden tours. "Gardening has always been with me," she says. ❧

▲ Perennial and rose borders soften the transition between the house and its garden. Liz loves the way the cheery yellow facade of her house and garage serve as a warm backdrop for her effervescent plantings.

Liz prefers ornamentation to be placed spontaneously rather than formally.

four seasons of green

an enduring naturalistic garden

an enduring naturalistic garden

T here's a sense that you're taking a long journey to a remote, secret place when you visit Anne Holt's waterfront garden. Towering second-growth Douglas firs and western red cedars soar above the worn gravel driveway curving through the grass. A natural understory of native saplings, ferns, salal, and other woodland volunteers thrives at eye level, progeny of shrubs and trees that germinated following the second logging of Bainbridge Island, more than a century ago. With trees that old, the property has a quality of depth and permanence rarely seen in urban gardens. A visitor once remarked that you don't *tour* Anne Holt's garden, you "wade through the essence" of it.

Emerging from the long driveway into a light-filled bowl of verdant green is well worth the journey. Anne's is a glorious, lively landscape

◄ ◄ A thoughtfully planted border features plants in every shade of green, growing in forms tall and short, leafy and needled, mounded and weeping.

◄ Perhaps because the grassy, single-lane drive is submerged in deep shade, the tiny angelic creature perched on a mossy stump seems like a shining gift to all who enter this garden.

▲ Weathered by time, an immense pair of hinged gates admits visitors to the walled garden.

▲ In springtime, when many branches are still bare, the strolling garden exudes fresh green growth. Anne uses the outer edges of the walled garden as a stage against which to present ornamental shrubs and half-moon beds of perennials and bulbs.

◄ Anne Holt shares her joyful spirit—and her garden—with many.

► Clockwise, from top left: Spring crocuses and other tiny bulbs thrive in the green roof of the outdoor sauna; Anne's cedar sauna house has a sod roof that helps the structure blend into the landscape; within the garden's spiral labyrinth, its walking path is exactly the width of the lawnmower, revealing the designer's pragmatism.

that reminds you of the inviting strolling gardens on old English estates. Yet the diversity of foliage, color, texture, and plant forms signals that this is more than a park: it's a plant-collector's living laboratory. Wide sections of lawn offer a pleasing contrast to dense hedgerows of deciduous and evergreen shrubs. Balanced among these elements are a secret walled garden and a spiral grass labyrinth, both of which evoke a sense of time standing still. Uniquely Northwest touches help define this place, including rustic carved tree stumps, a cedar sauna (inspired by Anne's fishing trips to Alaska's Kenai Peninsula) with turf growing on its roof, and refreshing views of Puget Sound extending beyond a gravel beach.

Anne always hoped to settle on the thirty-six-square-mile island. "I used to come here as a child in the summertime," she says. "Once I was married, my husband and I searched for a piece of land. We packed up the kids—we had two, and I was pregnant with a third child—and came on over to look for property."

That was in 1953. Anne and her husband, Irving Clark Jr., were visiting friends on Bainbridge Island when a neighbor came over with an armload of roses and mentioned she was selling her home next ▶ **165**

timelessness

When the garden and
gardener put down roots
in a place, the result is
an enduring landscape.

I f one has been able to grow and tend a
garden for ten years—or for several decades—
its aura of timelessness may seem to have
been effortlessly achieved. When we enter a
garden with an ageless character, we often
respond first to the mood or the atmosphere.
A sense of calm and respite permeates a
timeless garden, welcoming visitors to an
otherworldly experience.

Architectural cues signify permanence
in such a landscape. When a house is well
connected with the garden, in proper
proportion with its surroundings, there's
an enduring and established quality to the
design. Living spaces are seamlessly linked
with outdoor spaces via deep porches,
French doors, window seats, and terraces.
Fences, trellises, and arbors are fabricated
with substantial rather than lightweight
timber. Vertical surfaces—walls and trellises—
are softened, by a partial covering of vines,
climbing plants, or shrubs trained into
patterned espaliers.

A timeless garden wraps itself around
home and inhabitants. Perhaps there is a
canopy overhead, one of big-leaf maples or
draping hemlock branches, filtering daylight

to give the garden a dreamy quality. Hedges
and borders are dense rather than sparse,
with branches and stems that companionably
link arms to suggest they've always grown in
that spot. Formal or informal, these walls of
green can be grown from deciduous trees or
evergreen shrubs—or a delightful
combination of both.

The boundaries between ornamental
borders and pathways are often blurred in a
timeless garden, due to a soft coloration of
mossy green. And underfoot, the earth is
cushioned with a variety of ground covers
and low-growing plants that seem magically
woven in place.

Since it's often not possible to begin a
garden with mature trees, instead suggest
permanence through the plants you select:
woody shrubs with a profusion of fragrant
flowers, trees with multiseason interest,
carefree vines that twist and twine, and long-
blooming perennials that begin in spring and
continue through autumn.

Materials and finishes that are appreciated
for their time-worn patinas are an ideal reflection
of permanence. A weathered wood bench
tucked in a cozy niche, rough cast-stone
vessels overflowing with ivy, rusted iron or
oxidized brass containers, and even art objects
with distressed paint—all convey history and
a sense of time. Rather than poured concrete
pathways or patios, surfaces such as crushed
rock, irregular or carefully pieced stepping-
stones, and recycled brick suggest age.

When the garden and gardener alike
put down roots in a place, the result is an
enduring and enchanting landscape. In such
a scenario, timelessness emanates more
from an evident reverence for the plants and
materials selected and from the spirit of your
garden than from the actual passage of time.

▲ The carefree *Clematis tangutica* graces an arbor, which Anne's son, Tom, fashioned from copper

piping. Flanked by delightful stone cherubs, the alluring portal leads to the distant lawn.

door. "We stepped through the fence and I knew right away that this was the place," Anne recalls. "We wanted a west-facing piece of property, on the water. It is just a miracle that we came here—it was a great gift."

Used primarily as a summer residence, the partially wooded six-acre parcel was undemanding, and initially Anne ignored the garden. "We didn't do anything to the property for years—we just came over and enjoyed it," she explains. But when Anne's husband died in 1979, she decided to move to Bainbridge Island permanently with her youngest child, then 16. She returned to school to study horticulture and landscape design, eventually opening a small garden design business and plant nursery on her property, called Agate Nursery.

Growing along with her design business, Anne's garden began to thrive as a living laboratory for all sorts of woody trees and shrubs. Active in the Seattle Rhododendron Society, Washington Park Arboretum, and the Washington Native Plant Society, Anne learned to propagate choice specimens for clients' projects, holding onto favorite plants for her expanding garden displays. "I wanted people who came here to see how things would look in a mature garden," she explains.

Thus, by necessity, Anne turned her passion for plants into a career. "By the time I thought about embellishing this property, I knew every corner—I knew where the light fell and where things would grow," she explains. This intimacy with the character of her garden informed many design choices, as Anne wove together textured borders of conifers and maples, azaleas, and woodland perennials.

A self-described "plantaholic," Anne says she is attracted to horticultural offerings from continents with conditions similar to her own sheltered Zone 8 microclimate. "Some of these plants are marginal—some have made it, some have not," she acknowledges. If it can be started from seed, propagated by cuttings, or increased by divisions, Anne is devoted to keeping alive generations of a special plant. Unique foliage and unusual plant forms are particularly alluring to this plantswoman. "Mother Nature does interesting things occasionally," she says, admitting to a love for exotica in the garden. "I call them 'witches'—plants with variations."

Her lavishly layered garden is by no means merely a collection of oddities and quirky plants. Against a timeless backdrop of mature trees and shrubs, a few choice specimens inspire tales of their heritage. There's an unnamed dogwood tree that flourishes with unusual five petal-like bracts. Anne brought it home in a coffee can, purchased for $3 at Seattle's Pike Place Market fifteen years ago. It now creates a delicate pink canopy along the north side of her garden.

"By the time I thought about embellishing this property, I knew every corner—I knew where the light fell and where things would grow."

▲ Branches, berries, and blooms from Anne's garden create lovely arrangements that celebrate services at Grace Episcopal Church.

◄ Clockwise, from top left: Scenes from Anne's woodland wonderland include: a deciduous azalea's fragrant gold-orange blooms; the *Clematis tangutica*'s four-pointed petals, accented by dark centers; a playful stone bunny emerging from the peony border; a bowl-shaped Japanese peony; a larger-than-life owl, carved into the remnant trunk of a felled tree; and a woodland toad lily (*Tricyrtis formosana*) with a lovely spotted pattern.

There's the Loderi rhododendron (*Rhododendron* 'Loderi King George')—the first she ever planted here in the 1960s—a gift from Brian Mulligan, the late director of Seattle's Washington Park Arboretum. The fragrant shrub has its pedigree in the Loderi Group of rhododendron hybrids raised in the early 1900s by British hybridizer Sir Edmund Loder. A russet apple tree's parentage dates back to the *Mayflower*, which Anne cherishes for its perennially tasty fruit.

Anne has experimented with just about every style of garden design, from formal to natural. She's raised mature specimens from seedlings and whips. She's turned hazardous trees into naturalistic artwork. She's enjoyed the freedom that comes from owning a large canvas on which to design a garden. Ornamental shrubs, trees with patterned bark and bright foliage, climbing vines with porcelain-like flowers—all are given room to grow, stretching their branches and tendrils without limits.

◄ Formed from woven branches and twigs, this ever-changing basket is filled with seasonal displays. Anne added playful touches of color by displaying blue glass bottles on stakes.

▲ A garden within a garden is encountered upon entering Anne's secluded, European-inspired sanctuary. Water bubbles in a classic urn, placed on crushed stone at the axis of the garden's formal quadrants.

Trees with patterned bark and bright foliage are given room to grow, stretching their branches without limits.

◄ A raven is silhouetted against the striated late-summer grasses.

▲ The many-hued foliage of one of Anne's many Japanese maples announces the advent of cooler fall temperatures.

The most formal element of this landscape is the walled garden. In 1990, after several tours of gardens in England, Ireland, and Italy, and influenced by centuries of European gardens, Anne erected a rectangular walled courtyard using split-face concrete blocks, finished in brick across the top. She credits longtime friend Penelope Hobhouse, the famous English garden maker, for inspiring the design. "I always wanted to come home from England with a castle or wall fragment," Anne jokes. "When Penny visited, we had her stand on a chair to help plan our own walled garden."

Hobhouse recommended using the lap pool's proportions to guide the enclosure's scale, placing it perpendicular to the fifty-foot-long swimming pool and patio. Ed Kopp, a carpenter from Seattle, fabricated the massive hinged gates using Alaskan yellow cedar planks. The gates provide access through the north and south walls of the garden. Once inside, you are transported to the British Isles.

With pathways of rosy crushed marble and sand lined with benches and urns, the walled garden creates its own microclimate. *Eucryphia cordifolia*, with creamy white spring blooms and glossy green ▶ 172

▲ Sunlight casts a golden glow on this dazzling tapestry of deciduous trees.

the timeless approach

For a seasoned look, remove the sense of newness.

To grow an abundant garden with a sense of timelessness in less than a lifetime, the goal is to unify and knit together areas of the garden, softening the edges and removing the sense of newness. Here are some guidelines.

Materials and Finishes: Hardscape materials that suggest a sense of age and rich character successfully communicate timelessness in the garden. The seasoned look of weathered rock, mossy wood, vine-draped trellises, and aged metal objects— all effective choices—can suggest they were placed here years before. Replace the shiny or glossy with galvanized or matte-finished surfaces; add interesting twigs and branches to adorn an ordinary arbor or gate; encourage ground covers to cushion the spaces between stepping stones or pavers.

Plants and Placement: We can intentionally select and place plants that fill a garden with timeless character. Borrow techniques from veteran landscape designers: Group several young trees in an inviting stand of three or five, instantly giving the grove a presence that a single tree couldn't offer. Grow informal layers of horizontal plants beneath vertical ones for complexity; the eye will see a pleasingly textured composition. Frame borrowed views from adjacent gardens, parks, greenbelts, or pastures. Direct pools of light into secreted grottos, either by placing columnar trees or shrubs at an entrance or by training vines over an archway.

Groundwork: Bare soil is an instant giveaway that a garden is young. Strike a balance between anticipating the ultimate size a shrub or tree may achieve in your garden (beginning with plants that seem too widely spaced) and planting everything so close together that your garden seems crowded. Be aware that later you may have to edit, thinning beds and borders as plants get larger. With perennials, you can integrate plants more densely, using a combination of tall, medium, and smaller choices. Add interest by moving dynamic vertical plants to the foreground, especially if you select open-form varieties that show off what's behind them. And wherever possible, plant ground covers that can do double-duty in the garden, suppressing weeds and masking bare soil. Woolly or creeping thymes (*Thymus pseudolanuginosus*; *T. praecox arcticus*), baby's tears (*Soleirolia soleirolii*), blue star creeper (*Pratia pedunculata*), creeping Jenny (*Lysimachia nummularia*), and stonecrop (various sedums) are among the many ground cover choices that will take root and seem timeless once established.

Adornments: Choose garden art and ornamentation with a timeless quality. Aged urns and planters give permanence in the landscape. Select objects carefully, letting the few you display harmonize rather than compete with the plants. Allow artworks to be partially obscured by branches, or encourage vines to grow nearby, like clematis, so tendrils will entwine the sculpture or artifact.

▲ A stone frog is nearly obscured by moss, ferns, and primulas.
▶ Buttery yellow poppies dance at the base of a multistemmed tree. Anne limbed up the tree's lower branches, turning its lichen-encrusted trunks into a naturalistic sculpture.

▲ The heavily veined and pleated gunnera thrives in moist soil at the pond's edge.

► Joined by a resident duck, a pair of lifelike cranes is mirrored in the pond. The figures add a natural touch to the woodland scene, where a weeping sequoia has fallen into the water.

"I didn't plant much, because I wanted to see what would come up naturally."

foliage, grows in each corner. *Camellia sasanqua* branches are trained along the outer walls, the winter blossoms providing a rosy contrast against the stone. Climbing hydrangea, roses, and trumpet vines lend a blanket of color and foliage. Peonies, roses, clematis—traditional blooms of the English garden—indeed belong here, as does the trim boxwood edging. This is a timeless sanctuary.

Along the southern border of her land, Anne once removed a row of fir and cedar trees that were threatening to destroy the lattice fence, paying her sons and their friends to chop the trees into firewood. "She planted rockspray, a climbing cotoneaster (*Cotoneaster horizontalis*) with distinctive herringbone-patterned branching, to cover the new fence. When the leaves drop off, the berries hang on. It's wonderfully colorful," she enthuses. Against this backdrop grow Japanese maples and rhododendron shrubs, statuesque and shading much of that side of the garden. "The trees have made this garden go from sunny to shady," she admits. A border of perennials—hostas, dwarf Japanese maples, *Franklinia*, and ground covers—flank a path that meanders through the trees.

Beyond the walled garden is Anne's pond, sited appropriately at a boggy spot that collects water runoff from the wooded area above. Thriving around its perimeter are sedges, gunnera, irises, and willows, lavishly growing together and obscuring the water's edge. "I didn't plant much, because I wanted to see what would come up naturally," she explains.

Having begun life as a whip cut from a felled tree elsewhere on the property, a stately willow dips its branch tips into the pond's surface. "It's a perfectly gorgeous feature that began when I just stuck it in the ground," Anne says. The otherworldly, water-loving gunnera plants thrive here, happily spreading their prehistoric leaves to shade tiny jewel-like primulas that grow at their feet.

When a weeping sequoia succumbed to age and toppled into the pond, Anne allowed it to remain there. "That sequoia was always leaning toward the sun, and it reached too far," she explains, with a knowing grin. Otters, turtles, and other wildlife frequently visit this natural bridge, welcomed by the pair of sculpted cranes that reside alongside it.

Anne says the best feature of her garden is the "part I haven't touched." With more than half of her property left undeveloped as nature's handiwork, she has given a conservation easement to the Bainbridge Island Land Trust. "It means I cannot do anything, cut any trees or remove anything from the area above the pond up to the road."

This ardent plantswoman and designer has cultivated an alluring garden legacy. The landscape is and will always be her venue for artistic expression. She continues to share this treasured place with friends and loyal horticultural visitors. Well into her retirement years, Anne has continued landscape design consulting, spending much of the past year creating a meditative garden for her new parish sanctuary. "Gardening is even more important to me," Anne says. "I'm concentrating on growing plants in pots that I can move around the house," she says. You can be sure those containers are an abundant, moveable feast for the eyes. ❧

index